ASSESSMENT

Chapter Tests

Second Course

- Reading
- Writing
- Sentences and Paragraphs
- Grammar, Usage, Mechanics

HOLT, RINEHART AND WINSTON

A Harcourt Classroom Education Company

Austin · New York · Orlando · Atlanta · San Francisco · Boston · Dallas · Toronto · London

STAFF CREDITS

EDITORIAL

Director
Mescal Evler

Manager of Editorial Operations
Bill Wahlgren

Executive Editors
Robert R. Hoyt
Emily G. Shenk

Project Editor
Cheryl L. Christian

Writing and Editing
Barbara Scroggie Knaggs
Rebecca Bennett
David Knaggs
Paige M. Leavitt
Kim Soriano, *Editorial Assistant*

Copyediting
Michael Neibergall, *Copyediting Manager;* Mary Malone, *Senior Copyeditor;* Joel Bourgeois, Elizabeth Dickson, Gabrielle Field, Jane Kominek, Millicent Ondras, Theresa Reding, Kathleen Scheiner, Laurie Schlesinger, *Copyeditors*

Project Administration
Marie Price, *Managing Editor;* Lori De La Garza, *Editorial Operations Coordinator;* Thomas Browne, Heather Cheyne, Diane Hardin, Mark Holland, Marcus Johnson, Jill O'Neal, Joyce Rector, Janet Riley, Kelly Tankersley, *Project Administration;* Gail Coupland, Ruth Hooker, Margaret Sanchez, *Word Processing*

Editorial Permissions
Janet Harrington, *Permissions Editor*

ART, DESIGN AND PHOTO

Graphic Services
Kristen Darby, *Manager*

Image Acquisitions
Joe London, *Director;* Tim Taylor, *Photo Research Supervisor;* Rick Benavides, *Assistant Photo Researcher;* Elaine Tate, *Supervisor;* Erin Cone, *Art Buyer*

Cover Design
Sunday Patterson

PRODUCTION
Belinda Barbosa Lopez, *Senior Production Coordinator*
Simira Davis, *Supervisor*
Nancy Hargis, *Media Production Supervisor*
Joan Lindsay, *Production Coordinator*
Beth Prevelige, *Prepress Manager*

MANUFACTURING
Michael Roche, *Supervisor of Inventory and Manufacturing*

Copyright © by Holt, Rinehart and Winston

All rights reserved. No part of this publication may be reproduced or transmitted in any form or by any means, electronic or mechanical, including photocopy, recording, or any information storage and retrieval system, without permission in writing from the publisher.

Teachers using ELEMENTS OF LANGUAGE may photocopy blackline masters in complete pages in sufficient quantities for classroom use only and not for resale.

Printed in the United States of America

ISBN 0-03-056379-8

4 5 085 04

Table of Contents

About These Tests v
Symbols for Revising and Proofreading vi

Communications

for PART 1
(Pupil's Edition pp. 1–271)

Chapter 1: Narration/Description
Sharing Your Life
    Reading Workshop 1
    Writing Workshop 4

Chapter 2: Exposition
Explaining a Complex Process
    Reading Workshop 7
    Writing Workshop 10

Chapter 3: Exposition
Explaining Cause and Effect
    Reading Workshop 13
    Writing Workshop 16

Chapter 4: Exposition
Analyzing a Book
    Reading Workshop 19
    Writing Workshop 22

Chapter 5: Exposition
Reporting Your Research
    Reading Workshop 25
    Writing Workshop 28

Chapter 6: Persuasion
Sharing an Opinion
    Reading Workshop 31
    Writing Workshop 34

Chapter 7: Persuasion
Using Brochures
    Reading Workshop 37
    Writing Workshop 42

Chapter Tests

Table of Contents

Sentences and Paragraphs

for PART 2
(Pupil's Edition pp. 272–319)

Chapter 8: Writing Effective Sentences 47

Chapter 9: Learning About Paragraphs 50

Grammar, Usage, and Mechanics

for PART 3
(Pupil's Edition pp. 320–751)

Chapter 10: The Sentence 53

Chapter 11: Parts of Speech Overview
   Noun, Pronoun, Adjective 56

Chapter 12: Parts of Speech Overview
   Verb, Adverb, Preposition, Conjunction, Interjection 59

Chapter 13: Complements 62

Chapter 14: The Phrase 65

Chapter 15: The Clause 68

Chapter 16: Sentence Structure 71

Chapter 17: Agreement 74

Chapter 18: Using Verbs Correctly 77

Chapter 19: Using Pronouns Correctly 80

Chapter 20: Using Modifiers Correctly 83

Chapter 21: A Glossary of Usage 86

Chapter 22: Capital Letters 89

Chapter 23: Punctuation
   End Marks, Commas, Semicolons, and Colons 92

Chapter 24: Punctuation
   Underlining (Italics), Quotation Marks, Apostrophes, Hyphens, Parentheses, Brackets, Dashes 95

Chapter 25: Spelling 98

Chapter 26: Correcting Common Errors 101

FOR THE TEACHER

About These Tests

Every chapter in your *Elements of Language* Pupil's Edition has an accompanying Chapter Test in traditional format. The Answer Keys for these tests are located in a separate booklet, *Test Answer Keys*.

Part 1 | **Communications**

The Part 1 tests include assessment for both the Reading and the Writing Workshops. You may choose to administer the Reading and Writing Workshop tests separately or as one test after students have completed the chapter.

In the **Reading Workshop** test, students read a passage, respond to short-answer questions, and complete a graphic organizer. The passage is in the mode that students have just studied, and the questions and the graphic organizer assess students' proficiency in the chapter's Reading Skill and Reading Focus.

The **Writing Workshop** test provides a passage containing problems or errors in several or all of the following areas: content, organization, style, grammar and usage, and mechanics. Students demonstrate their understanding of the mode of writing and their revising and proofreading skills by revising the essay and correcting the errors. A Revising Guidelines page reminds students of the chapter skills and the basic requirements of the chapter writing mode.

To help students complete the Writing Workshop tests, you may want to give them photocopies of the following page, which lists symbols for revising and proofreading.

Part 2 | **Sentences and Paragraphs**

The Part 2 tests provide assessment for each major section within the Sentences and Paragraphs chapters. Students complete exercises similar to those in the Pupil's Edition. These exercises test students' mastery of the key concepts taught in the chapters.

Part 3 | **Grammar, Usage, and Mechanics**

The Part 3 tests provide assessment for the rules and key concepts taught in the grammar, usage, and mechanics chapters in the Pupil's Edition. Students demonstrate their mastery of the instruction by completing a variety of tests that are similar to the exercises in the Pupil's Edition.

Chapter Tests

Symbols for Revising and Proofreading

The following symbols will help you revise and correct the passages in the Writing Workshop tests.

SYMBOL	DEFINITION	EXAMPLE
⌒	Delete word.	The girl smiled ~~at me~~.
∧	Insert.	The girl smiled ∧. (at me)
⁄	Replace a word.	I found the ~~book~~. (record)
≡	Set in capital letters.	Does karen like fish?
/	Set in lowercase.	Does Karen /Like /Fish?
˸	Insert apostrophe.	Its his dog.
ˮ	Insert quotation marks.	It's his dog, he said.
⊙	Insert period.	If she goes, I go⊙
˸	Insert comma.	If she goes I go.
⊙	Insert colon.	Pick a color˸ red, blue, or green.
⁏	Insert semicolon.	We went⁏ she stayed.

ELEMENTS OF LANGUAGE | Second Course

| NAME | CLASS | DATE | SCORE |

for **CHAPTER 1** *page 18*   **TEST**

Reading Workshop: Personal Narrative

DIRECTIONS Read the following passage, and answer the questions in the right-hand column.

The Expert

I joined a caving club when I moved to Blacksburg. These cavers were old friends, a fairly exclusive bunch of buddies, and after a year, I was still the newest, slowest, most cautious member of the group.

I was surprised then to get a call from Jim one Saturday: "I wondered whether you'd like to explore Lynx with us tomorrow."

I was elated. Usually I invited myself. I must finally be good enough! They wanted me!

Jim continued, "Kathy's coming over from Richmond, and I'd like to take her, but I think she'd feel more comfortable with another woman along."

Oh! Then I thought of the bright side: I would be the experienced one. Poor Kathy, little did she know the cold, darkness, mud, and danger that lay before her, but I would be there.

"Sure," I said, "I'd love to."

We met at the entrance—Jim, Kathy, and four other cavers. I was wearing coveralls over my long johns, an ugly green wool sweater with moth holes, a long muffler, and two pairs of socks. Kathy looked quite stylish; it was obvious that she hadn't dressed warmly enough, poor thing. Well, we would bring her out early if we needed to.

Once inside, with our carbide lamps lighting the way, I felt better. Lynx was a beautiful cave, and Jim was taking us on the scenic route. Kathy stopped to admire a stalactite. I saw my chance.

"You know how these are formed?" I began.

"Yes," said Kathy.

1. What feelings does the writer describe up to this point?

_____

_____

_____

_____

Chapter Tests   **1**

for CHAPTER 1 page 18 continued   TEST

As I was thinking up a witty reply, Jim said, "Let's do the canyon." I couldn't believe my ears. I had never climbed the canyon; surely it was impossible for a newcomer like Kathy.

To get to the canyon we had to cross a drop. The sides looked slippery. Jim took a wide step and was over, then Kathy, then the others. I looked down and froze.

"I, uh, need a belay," squeaked a tiny voice from inside my throat. A belay is a safety rope. My legs seemed to have shrunk. Mike tossed me a rope, and not looking down, I went over.

In the canyon, two high walls came together in a V-shape. We held ourselves up between the walls with our knees, hands, elbows, and feet, and carefully inched along. The bottom of the canyon was far below.

Gradually the walls opened out. Ahead of me the others, including Kathy, kept working their way along. I couldn't figure out how they were doing it. My body would not cooperate. I inched backward, and squeaked again.

"I'll stay with her," Mike said. (You never leave someone alone in a cave.) In what seemed like hours later they came back, raving about the underground river I'd always wanted to see. Kathy was glowing.

Outside the cave, I handed my track sheet to Jim. I was still working toward membership in the club, and every expedition counted. Kathy tried to look over his shoulder as he wrote something in the Comments box and handed it back to me.

"So did you make progress?" she asked cheerfully.

I glanced at Jim's handwriting. "No significant progress, actually," I said, thinking to myself, "But I did learn a lesson: Pride goeth before a fall."

2. What begins to change for the writer once the group decides to explore the canyon?
_____
_____
_____
_____
_____

3. What details in the paragraphs about climbing the canyon show the writer's feelings?
_____
_____
_____
_____
_____
_____
_____

4. Is the writer's purpose to inform, to influence, to express, or to entertain?
_____
_____
_____
_____
_____

5. What, do you think, was the significance of this experience to the writer? Why?
_____
_____
_____
_____
_____
_____

2   ELEMENTS OF LANGUAGE | Second Course

NAME _____ CLASS _____ DATE _____

for **CHAPTER 1** *page 18* continued **TEST**

DIRECTIONS Use the ideas and information in the passage you have just read to complete the graphic organizer.

Identifying the Implied Main Idea

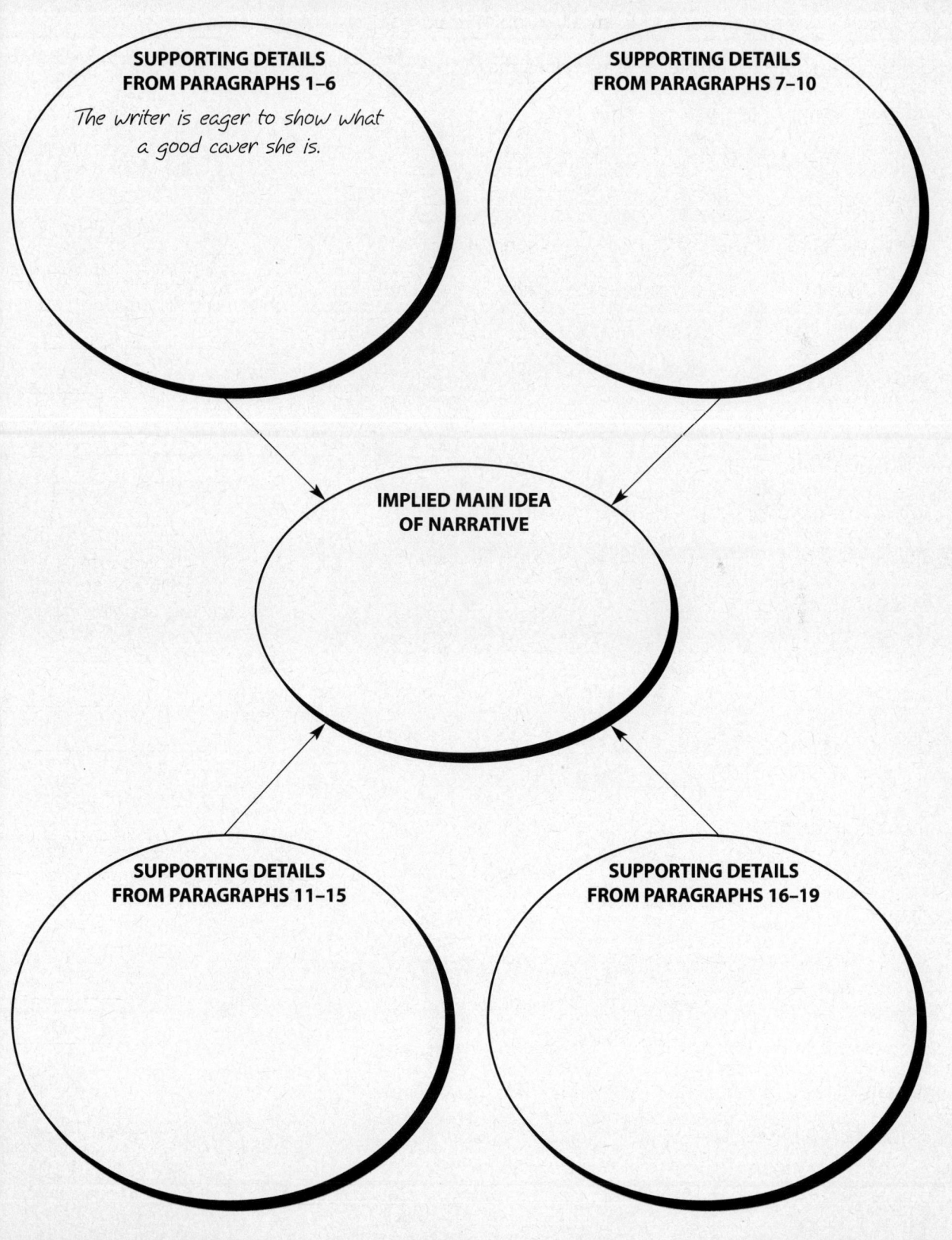

SUPPORTING DETAILS FROM PARAGRAPHS 1–6

The writer is eager to show what a good caver she is.

SUPPORTING DETAILS FROM PARAGRAPHS 7–10

IMPLIED MAIN IDEA OF NARRATIVE

SUPPORTING DETAILS FROM PARAGRAPHS 11–15

SUPPORTING DETAILS FROM PARAGRAPHS 16–19

Chapter Tests 3

NAME _____ CLASS _____ DATE _____

for **CHAPTER 1** *page 27*

REVISING GUIDELINES

Writing Workshop: Personal Narrative

DIRECTIONS Use the following guidelines to help you revise and correct the narrative on the next page.

THE INTRODUCTION SHOULD
- grab the audience's attention
- set the scene with details

▼

THE BODY SHOULD
- order events chronologically
- include details that make the people, places, and events seem real
- include thoughts and feelings

▼

THE CONCLUSION SHOULD
- state the meaning of the experience

REMEMBER TO
- ❑ avoid stringy sentences
- ❑ correctly use and punctuate dialogue

4   ELEMENTS OF LANGUAGE | Second Course

| NAME | CLASS | DATE | SCORE |

for **CHAPTER 1** page 27   **TEST**

Writing Workshop: Revising and Proofreading

DIRECTIONS The following personal narrative was written in response to this prompt:

Write about a memorable experience that you would not mind sharing.

The essay contains problems in style, content, and punctuation.

- Use the space between the lines to revise the paper and correct the errors.
- If you cannot fit some of your revisions between the lines, rewrite the revised sections on a separate piece of paper.

Learning Limits

When I was thirteen years old, I visited my uncle Joe's farm with my parents. I learned a lot from a mistake I made when I was there.   **a.** Problem with opening

I was excited to visit Uncle Joe because he had horses, and I had never ridden a horse before. Unfortunately, Uncle Joe told me that I couldn't ride by myself until he felt I had learned the basics. The first few days he led me around on his horse Snicker, showing me how to mount and dismount and how to use the reins to steer the horse. After three days, I was impatient to ride on my own.

The next morning I awoke at dawn and sneaked out to the barn. I managed to get the saddle and bridle on Snicker, and I led him out of the barn to the wooden rails of the paddock, and I climbed onto   **b.** Problem with stringy sentence the second rung to get my foot into the stirrup so I could mount. Once on top of the horse, I felt in complete control. We headed for the open field.

Chapter Tests   **5**

Snicker walked slowly at first. Then, as if to test me, he picked up the pace, and before I knew it, we were at a full gallop. No matter how hard I pulled on the reins, Snicker wouldn't slow down. I was scared. I yelled and held on to the reins.

c. Problem with details

My yelling attracted the attention of Uncle Joe and my parents, who were eating breakfast. They ran out of the house. When Uncle Joe saw Snicker galloping across the field, he whistled. Snicker, trained to obey Uncle Joe, turned back toward the house at a more leisurely pace. When I finally got back to the house, I was shaking. My dad looked up at me as I slumped in the saddle.

Son, he said, I don't think I need to tell you that was a dangerous stunt you just pulled.

d. Problem with punctuation

Now I don't pull dangerous stunts like that.

e. Problem with conclusion

NAME _____ CLASS _____ DATE _____ SCORE _____

for **CHAPTER 2** page 50

TEST

Reading Workshop: Complex Process

DIRECTIONS Read the following passage, and answer the questions in the right-hand column.

How Submarines Submerge and Resurface

These heavy, steel structures slowly rise and then quietly sink back into the ocean's depths. Their stealth and technology make them outstanding military and exploratory vessels. How do they do it?

For a submarine to descend, the crew in the control room of the vessel must increase the amount of water in containers called ballast tanks. These are located between the inner and outer hulls of the vessel. (A hull is the protective shell around the body of a submarine.) To increase the amount of water in the tanks, the crew must first open the large valves—called kingstons—at the bottom of the ballast tanks. As the water flows in, valves—called vents—located at the top of the tanks are opened and air escapes. As the ballast tanks fill with water, the vessel sinks deeper. When the crew reaches the desired depth, they close the kingstons.

When the crew is ready to resurface, they must fill the tanks with air instead of water. To do this, they first close the vents on top of the ballast tanks. Once the vents are closed, the crew uses controls to force pressurized air into the tanks. The pressure forces the kingstons on the bottom of the tanks open, and water is pushed out. The submarine's density decreases, and the submarine slowly rises to the water's surface.

1. Why do you think stealth is an important quality for a military vessel?
   _____
   _____
   _____
   _____

2. Why does the submarine sink deeper when more water enters the tanks?
   _____
   _____
   _____
   _____
   _____

3. What is the first step in making a submarine rise?
   _____
   _____
   _____
   _____

4. What causes the submarine's density to decrease?
   _____
   _____
   _____
   _____
   _____

Chapter Tests

7

Submarines have reached depths of 2,800 feet and remained underwater for months at a time. Their ability to maneuver at different depths and speeds makes them important military, exploratory, and research vessels.

5. Why would exploratory and research submarines need the same ability to sink to great ocean depths as military submarines do?

_____

_____

_____

_____

_____

NAME _____ CLASS _____ DATE _____

for CHAPTER 2 | page 50 | *continued* **TEST**

DIRECTIONS Use the ideas and information in the passage you have just read to complete the graphic organizer.

Finding Chronological Order

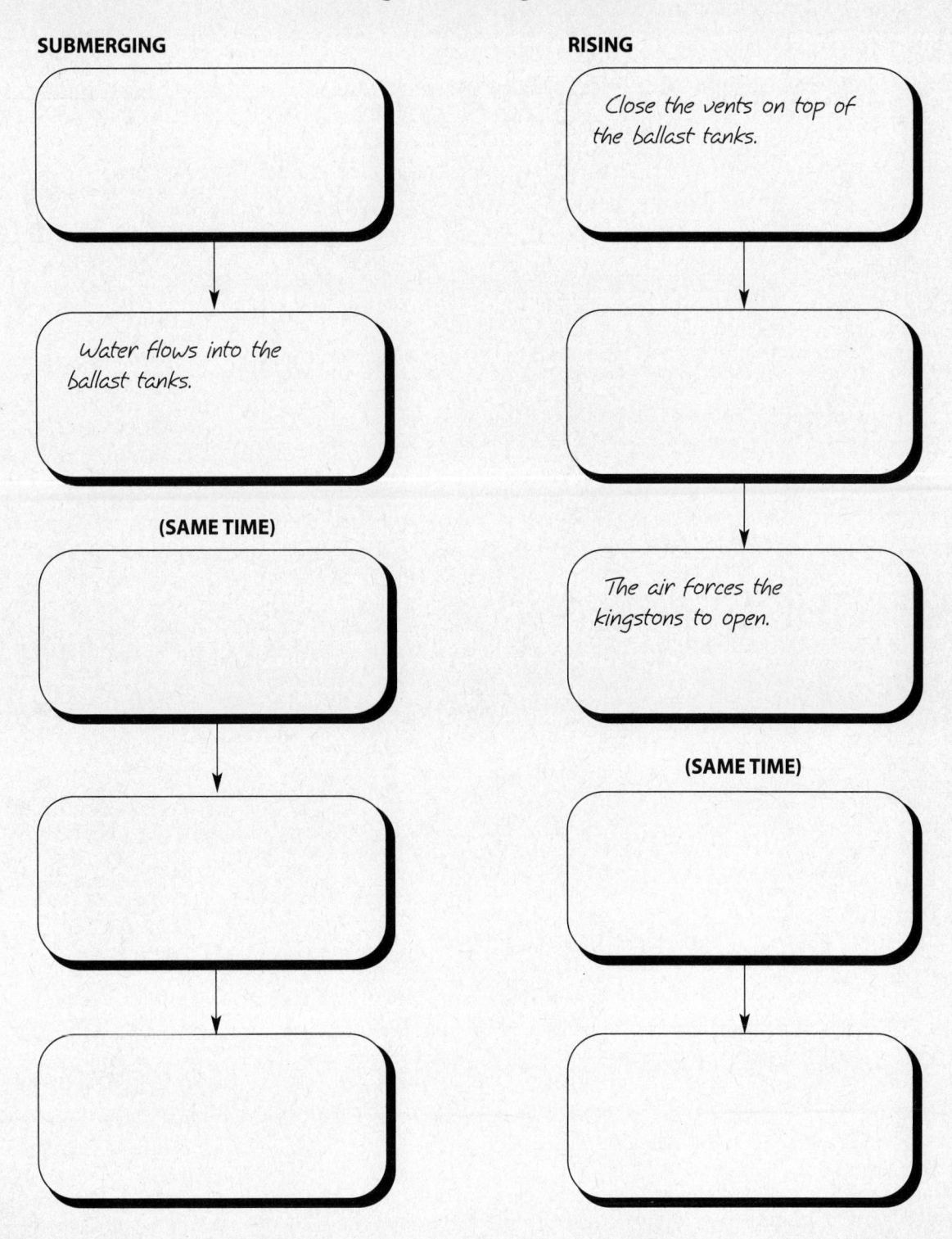

SUBMERGING

[ ]

↓

[Water flows into the ballast tanks.]

(SAME TIME)

[ ]

↓

[ ]

RISING

[Close the vents on top of the ballast tanks.]

↓

[ ]

↓

[The air forces the kingstons to open.]

(SAME TIME)

[ ]

↓

[ ]

Chapter Tests 9

NAME _____ CLASS _____ DATE _____

for **CHAPTER 2** | page 58 | **REVISING GUIDELINES**

Writing Workshop: Complex Process

DIRECTIONS Use the following guidelines to help you revise and correct the report on the next page.

THE INTRODUCTION SHOULD
- give readers a reason to learn about the process
- provide a clear topic statement
- include any necessary background information

▼

THE BODY SHOULD
- list steps in chronological order
- provide enough elaboration for each step to make each step of the process clear
- provide transitions to give the essay coherence and help show a logical progression of ideas

▼

THE CONCLUSION SHOULD
- make a final comment about the process and/or a restatement of its importance

---

REMEMBER TO
- ❏ use precise words
- ❏ use proper punctuation with introductory words and phrases

10   ELEMENTS OF LANGUAGE | Second Course

NAME _____ CLASS _____ DATE _____ SCORE _____

for **CHAPTER 2** page 58

TEST

Writing Workshop: Revising and Proofreading

DIRECTIONS The following report was written in response to this prompt:

> **Write a report explaining a complex process.**

The report contains problems in content, style, and punctuation.
- Use the space between the lines to revise the paper and correct the errors.
- If you cannot fit some of your revisions between the lines, rewrite the revised sections on a separate piece of paper.

How Honey Is Made

Honey is a delicious, natural sweetener that people enjoy in tea and desserts, and on toast. Have you ever wondered where honey comes from?

a. Problem with topic statement

Bees make honey to serve as their food. Although there are three types of honeybees in a colony—the queen, the drones, and the worker bees—only the worker bees build the honeycombs and make the honey. The bees' first task in making honey is to locate nectar, the sweet fluid in many flowers. Nectar is the primary ingredient in honey. Once they find it, the bees use their tube-shaped tongues to collect the nectar from flowers.

The nectar is stored in a honey stomach, a special compartment inside the bee's body. Special chemicals inside the bee's stomach turn the nectar into honey. Bees deposit the honey into the cells of the honeycomb where evaporation and the warmth of the hive remove the excess water from the honey.

b. Problem with transitions

Chapter Tests

11

Finally all that is left to do is harvest the honey. Bees use the hair on their hind legs to form small basket-like shapes that allow them to take the honey from the cells to eat. Humans, on the other hand, must remove the entire honeycomb, and allow the honey to come out of the cells.

All aspects of a bee's life, from the organization of the hive to the special features of its body, are focused on one thing—the production of honey.

c. Problem with punctuation

d. Problem with vague words

e. Problem with final comment

NAME _____ CLASS _____ DATE _____ SCORE _____

for **CHAPTER 3** page 84

TEST

Reading Workshop: Cause-and-Effect Article

DIRECTIONS Read the following passage, and answer the questions in the right-hand column.

The Story of Hail

Imagine you are visiting a farm in Wyoming on a sunny spring day. The lawn is shaded, and wheat gently sways in the fields. You go inside for an afternoon nap and awake to a deafening racket and a new landscape. The trees are bare, and the wheat is covered with ice. What happened? Did you sleep through spring and awaken in winter? Actually, you experienced a hailstorm, a downpour of frozen ice pellets that can cause serious crop and property damage.

How Hail Forms

Hail, small balls of ice that form within clouds, occurs when water droplets get swept into the updraft of a storm cloud. The droplets are pulled high into the cloud, where the temperature is below the freezing point (32 degrees Fahrenheit), and they instantly freeze, creating ice crystals. The ice crystals then bounce around in updrafts and downdrafts, collecting more and more water droplets and becoming larger and larger hailstones. When a hailstone becomes too heavy for the updraft to support, gravity takes over, and the stone falls to the ground.

The strength of the updraft affects how large a hailstone becomes. Clouds with updrafts of about 20 miles per hour produce pea-sized stones. Softball-sized stones require 100 mile-per-hour updrafts. As long as the updrafts and downdrafts are strong enough to suspend the hail, individual stones continue to grow. This is why the largest hailstones often arrive just before a tornado, which has powerful updrafts.

1. Based on the two heads in the passage, what questions does this passage answer?

_____
_____
_____
_____
_____

2. What causes hailstones to fall to the ground?

_____
_____
_____
_____
_____

3. What determines the size of a hailstone?

_____
_____
_____
_____
_____

Chapter Tests

13

Damage from Hailstorms

Falling hailstones, depending on size and prevailing winds, can travel at speeds up to 90 miles per hour. Hailstones traveling at this speed can, in just minutes, strip trees of their leaves and destroy farm crops. These dangerous hailstones can even harm livestock.

Hailstorms can also cause severe property damage. Roofs and cars look as though they've been pounded with a hammer. Hailstones can also shatter windows and windshields.

Despite the extensive damage associated with hail, it doesn't get the publicity that hurricanes, tornadoes, and blizzards get. It's not likely that hail will ever be the subject of a feature film as these other weather conditions have been, but experiencing one hailstorm is generally enough to convince anyone of the potential for destruction contained in these odd little—and not so little—balls of ice.

4. What effect is described in the first paragraph under this head?

5. What effect is described in the second paragraph under this head?

NAME _____ CLASS _____ DATE _____

for CHAPTER 3 page 84 *continued* **TEST**

DIRECTIONS Use the ideas and information in the passage you have just read to complete the graphic organizer.

Finding Causes and Effects

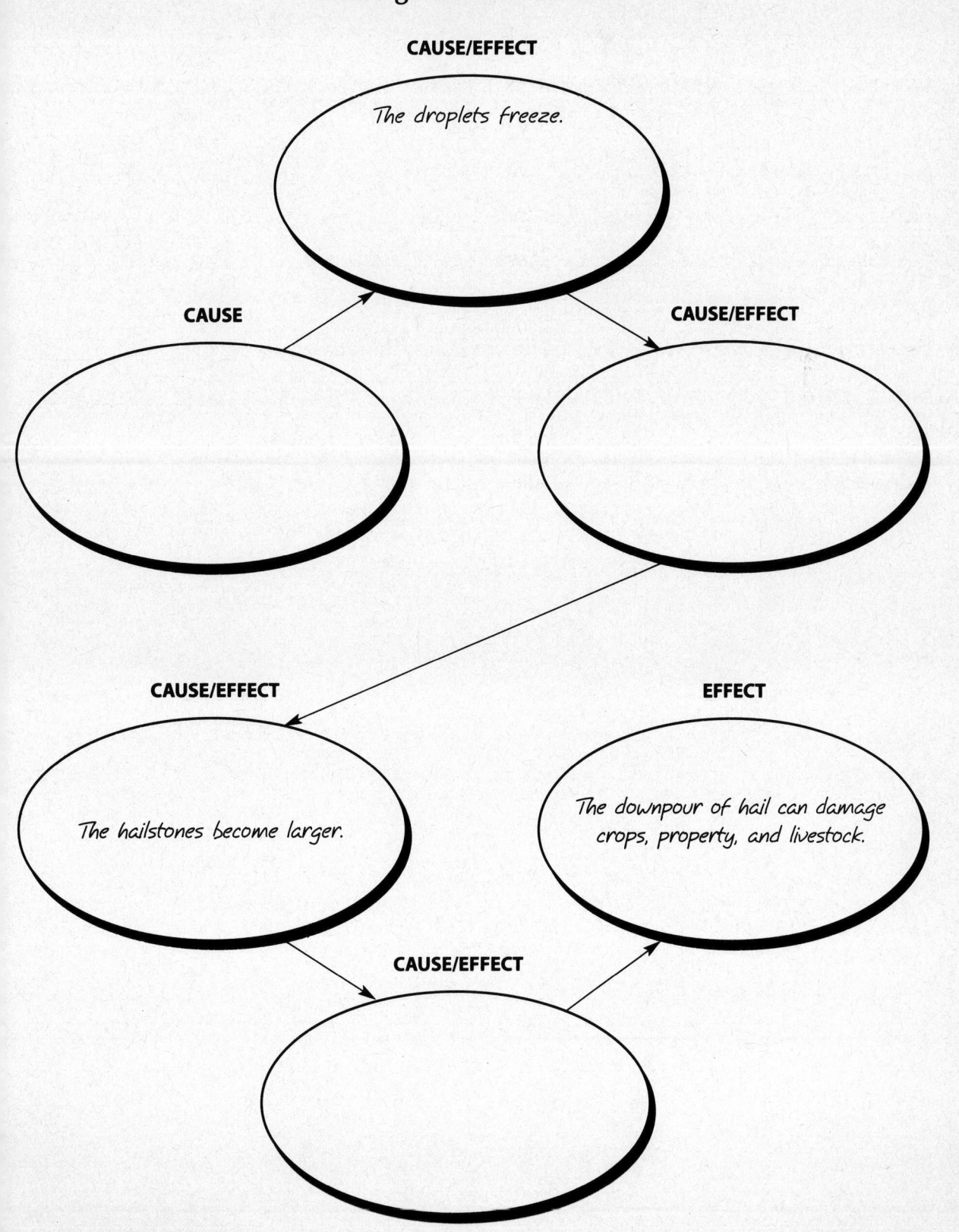

CAUSE/EFFECT

The droplets freeze.

CAUSE

CAUSE/EFFECT

CAUSE/EFFECT

The hailstones become larger.

EFFECT

The downpour of hail can damage crops, property, and livestock.

CAUSE/EFFECT

Chapter Tests

15

NAME _____ CLASS _____ DATE _____

for **CHAPTER 3** page 97

REVISING GUIDELINES

Writing Workshop: Cause-and-Effect Essay

DIRECTIONS Use the following guidelines to help you revise and correct the essay on the next page.

THE INTRODUCTION SHOULD
- grab the reader's attention
- include a main idea statement that identifies the cause-and-effect relationship
- include definitions and/or background information

▼

THE BODY SHOULD
- make sense to a younger audience
- contain paragraphs that each discuss one cause or one effect
- include enough logical support for each cause or effect
- include transitions to help ideas flow together coherently

▼

THE CONCLUSION SHOULD
- summarize the essay's main points or restate its main idea

REMEMBER TO
- ❑ use verbs in the active voice
- ❑ use colons and semicolons properly

16   ELEMENTS OF LANGUAGE | Second Course

| NAME | CLASS | DATE | SCORE |

for **CHAPTER 3**   page 97   **TEST**

Writing Workshop: Revising and Proofreading

DIRECTIONS The following essay was written in response to this prompt:

> Write a cause-and-effect essay about a health-related topic. Your audience will be younger readers.

The essay contains problems in content, style, and punctuation.

- Use the information in the **Databank** on the next page to help you with the revisions.
- Use the space between the lines to revise the paper and correct the errors.
- If you cannot fit some of your revisions between the lines, rewrite the revised sections on a separate piece of paper.

Running on Empty

People have many excuses for skipping breakfast. Some feel they do not have time for it; others skip the meal because they think it will help them lose weight.

> **a.** Problem with main idea statement

Missing the first meal of the day affects the level of nutrients in a body. After a night of sleep, the body has gone an average of ten hours without food. Already low glucose levels are caused to drop even lower when breakfast is skipped. With no food in the morning, the body has little energy. In addition, missing out on breakfast makes it difficult for people to eat the recommended daily amounts of vitamins and minerals.

> **b.** Problem with voice of verb

Breakfast jump-starts the metabolism (the rate at which the body burns calories). Without breakfast, the metabolism slows down to make calories and nutrients stored in the body last longer, people who frequently skip breakfast to reduce calories end up lowering their metabolism. This is one reason breakfast skippers are likely to

> **c.** Problem with punctuation

Chapter Tests   **17**

gain weight. Eating in the morning keeps the metabolism burning calories efficiently.

Families who skip breakfast miss out on an opportunity to start the day together. A family breakfast is also a great way to teach a child healthful eating habits. If adults are skipping breakfast, children learn to do the same.

Studies show that not eating breakfast can hurt students' school performance.

> **d.** Problem with logical support

Breakfast can be a quick piece of toast and fruit or an elaborate sit-down meal. Making breakfast a habit is easy, and it can even help students do better in school. Skipping breakfast, on the other hand, can hurt students' school performance and overall level of nutrition and cause them to miss the chance to start the day with their families.

DATABANK
- Students who eat breakfast score better on tests than students who do not eat breakfast.
- Skipping breakfast makes it harder for students to recall information.
- Skipping breakfast affects students' ability to use verbal skills.
- Skipping breakfast affects students' ability to control muscle coordination.
- Students who skip breakfast tire more quickly and become more irritable than students who eat breakfast.

| NAME | CLASS | DATE | SCORE |

for **CHAPTER 4** page 118   **TEST**

Reading Workshop: Book Review

DIRECTIONS Read the following review, and answer the questions in the right-hand column.

The Story of Robots

Why would anyone build a mechanical cockroach? Could scientists some day create an artificial being that acts and develops like a human being? In Ingrid Wickelgren's *Ramblin' Robots: Building a Breed of Mechanical Beasts*, readers get an entertaining history of the art and science of robotics and a look at what some roboticists think the future may hold for their creations. Packed with interesting facts, colorful anecdotes, and photographs, this book entertains and informs young adult readers who are interested in how—and why—people, animals, and robots behave in certain ways.

The book begins with a look at the earliest "robots," the automatons of the 1700s, and follows robot development from the invention of electronics to theories of artificial intelligence. The term *artificial intelligence* refers to "the science of making machines exhibit behavior that would be considered intelligent if performed by a human," and it has historically been a controversial subject. The author of *Ramblin' Robots* outlines the disagreement clearly and objectively to let the reader consider the possibility and desirability of creating humanoid robots.

Because robotics is a complicated field with its own specialized vocabulary, the author includes a glossary and uses examples from daily life to illustrate technical concepts. To demonstrate the principle of active balance, she uses the example of balancing a poster tube on one's palm. If the person doing this stays absolutely still, the object will fall; if his or her hand moves so that for every tipping in one direction, there is an equal tipping in the opposite direction, the object will remain upright. Throughout the book, the author offers

1. Who does the reviewer think is the likely audience for the book?

_____
_____
_____
_____

2. What does the second paragraph tell you about the content of the book?

_____
_____
_____
_____
_____

3. In the third paragraph, what aspect of the book does the reviewer evaluate? What is the evaluation?

_____
_____
_____
_____
_____

Chapter Tests   **19**

interesting, common-sense explanations of technical theories that educate readers.

The clear and direct language in *Ramblin' Robots* is appropriate for readers in middle school as well as readers who are older. Those who read it will find this book informative without being dull and entertaining without being silly.

4. Why does the reviewer believe that this book will interest a young audience?

_____
_____
_____
_____
_____

NAME _____ CLASS _____ DATE _____

for **CHAPTER 4** page 118 continued

TEST

DIRECTIONS Use the ideas and information in the passage you have just read to complete the graphic organizer.

Evaluating a Book Review

EVALUATION STANDARDS	SUMMARIZE WHAT THE REVIEWER SAYS
Audience Which group of readers will benefit from the book?	
Does the book's language and level fit the audience?	
Voice What tone does the author of the book use?	*The tone is clear and objective.*
Does the book keep readers interested?	
What example from the book shows the author's voice?	*The example showing how the author explains active balance demonstrates the author's common-sense voice.*
Content What kind of information is in the book?	
What references are made to helpful features in the book?	
How is the information in the book organized?	

Chapter Tests

for **CHAPTER 4** page 126

REVISING GUIDELINES

Writing Workshop: Book Review

DIRECTIONS Use the following guidelines to help you revise and correct the review on the next page.

THE INTRODUCTION SHOULD
- hook the reader's attention
- include a summary that gives the title, the author, and the topic of the book
- make a recommendation based on the most important evaluation standard

▼

THE BODY SHOULD
- include an evaluation statement for each of the three standards: audience, voice, and content
- include supporting evidence for each evaluation statement

▼

THE CONCLUSION SHOULD
- restate the original recommendation from the introduction, using different words

REMEMBER TO
- ❏ use adjective clauses to avoid short, choppy sentences
- ❏ punctuate essential and nonessential clauses correctly

| NAME | CLASS | DATE | SCORE |

for **CHAPTER 4** page 126   **TEST**

Writing Workshop: Revising and Proofreading

DIRECTIONS The following review was written in response to this prompt:

Review a book based on historical events.

The review contains problems in content, style, and punctuation.

- Choose from the information in the **Databank** on the next page to help you with the revisions.
- Use the space between the lines to revise the paper and correct the errors.
- If you cannot fit some of your revisions between the lines, rewrite the revised sections on a separate piece of paper.

Trails of Adventure

Imagine traveling over seven hundred miles on horseback in two weeks. Now imagine taking the journey as a young child—without any adults. In this book, readers experience the thrill of the journey as they take to the trails with Bud and Temp. Readers travel back in time and across the United States as they follow the six wild rides of brothers Bud and Temp Abernathy. This true adventure story is perfect for young adult readers.

a. Problem with summary

Bud & Me, written by Temp's wife Alta, traces the travels of the Abernathy brothers between 1909 and 1913. Cattle rustlers, horse-drawn fire wagons, and historical figures such as President Theodore Roosevelt appear. Alta Abernathy includes photographs. Alta Abernathy includes newspaper clippings. Alta Abernathy includes annotations. Alta Abernathy adds these three things to help bring this true story to life.

b. Problem with sentence style

This book is especially appealing to younger readers.

c. Problem with evidence

Although the book was written by Temp's wife Alta, it is told from Temp's point of view. The clear and simple language of this story which pulls readers in and places them directly on the trail never sounds childish. The author perfectly captures the voice of a brave and curious young traveler.

d. Problem with punctuation

Chapter Tests   **23**

This true adventure story is perfect for young adult readers. Temp's words sum it up best, "We were just little boys, but little boys with eyes wide open and minds ready to examine and absorb everything new."

e. Problem with recommendation

DATABANK
- Bud is nine and Temp is just five years old when they make their first trip. The vivid descriptions of the journey and the time period are very interesting.

NAME _____ CLASS _____ DATE _____ SCORE _____

for **CHAPTER 5** page 158

TEST

Reading Workshop: Informative Web Site

DIRECTIONS Read the following passage, and write your answers to the questions.

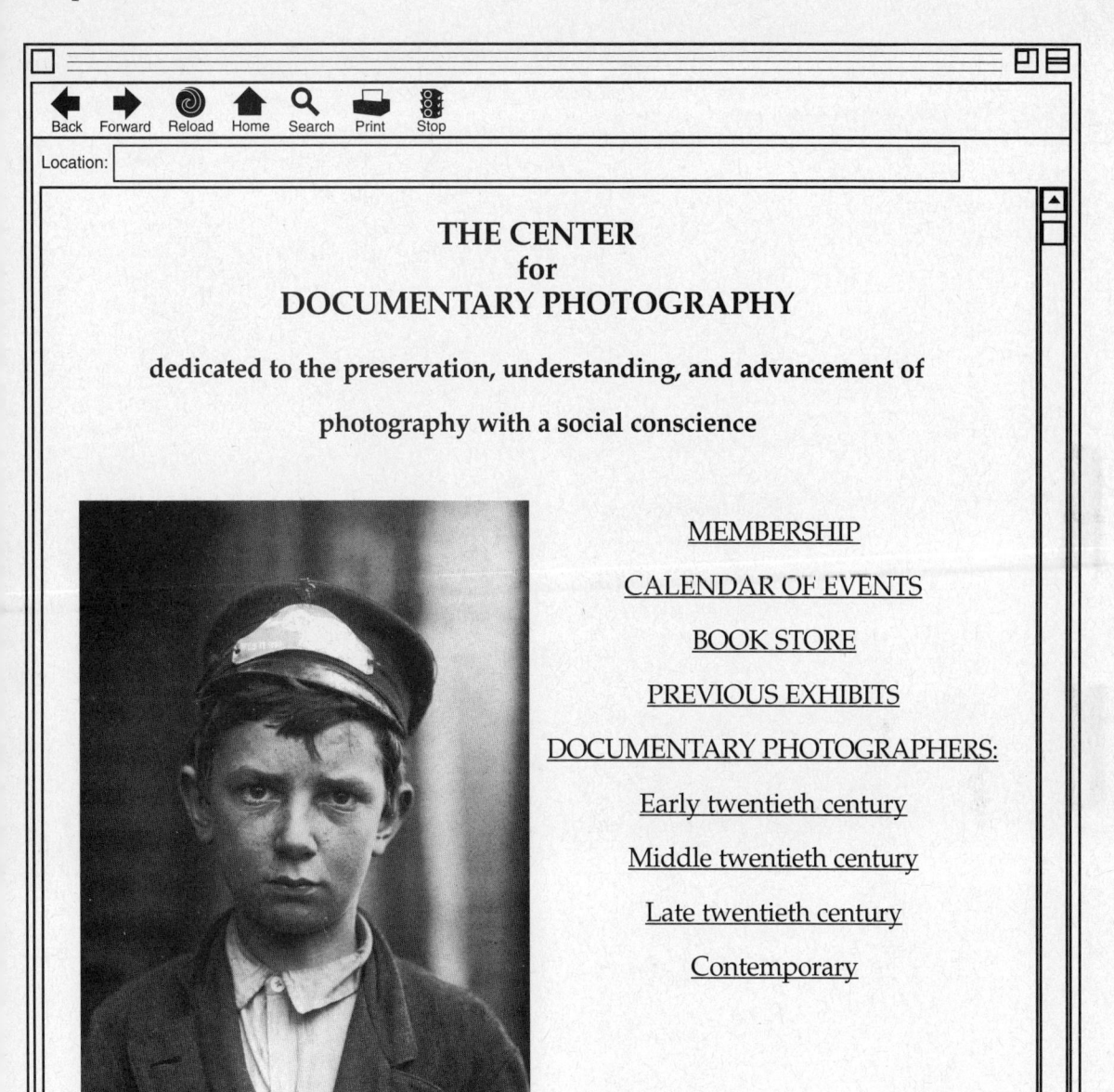

THE CENTER for DOCUMENTARY PHOTOGRAPHY

dedicated to the preservation, understanding, and advancement of photography with a social conscience

MEMBERSHIP

CALENDAR OF EVENTS

BOOK STORE

PREVIOUS EXHIBITS

DOCUMENTARY PHOTOGRAPHERS:

Early twentieth century

Middle twentieth century

Late twentieth century

Contemporary

Welcome to the Center for Documentary Photography home page. Click on a link above to begin.

1. Which of the links would likely lead to a list of upcoming exhibits?

_____

_____

Chapter Tests **25**

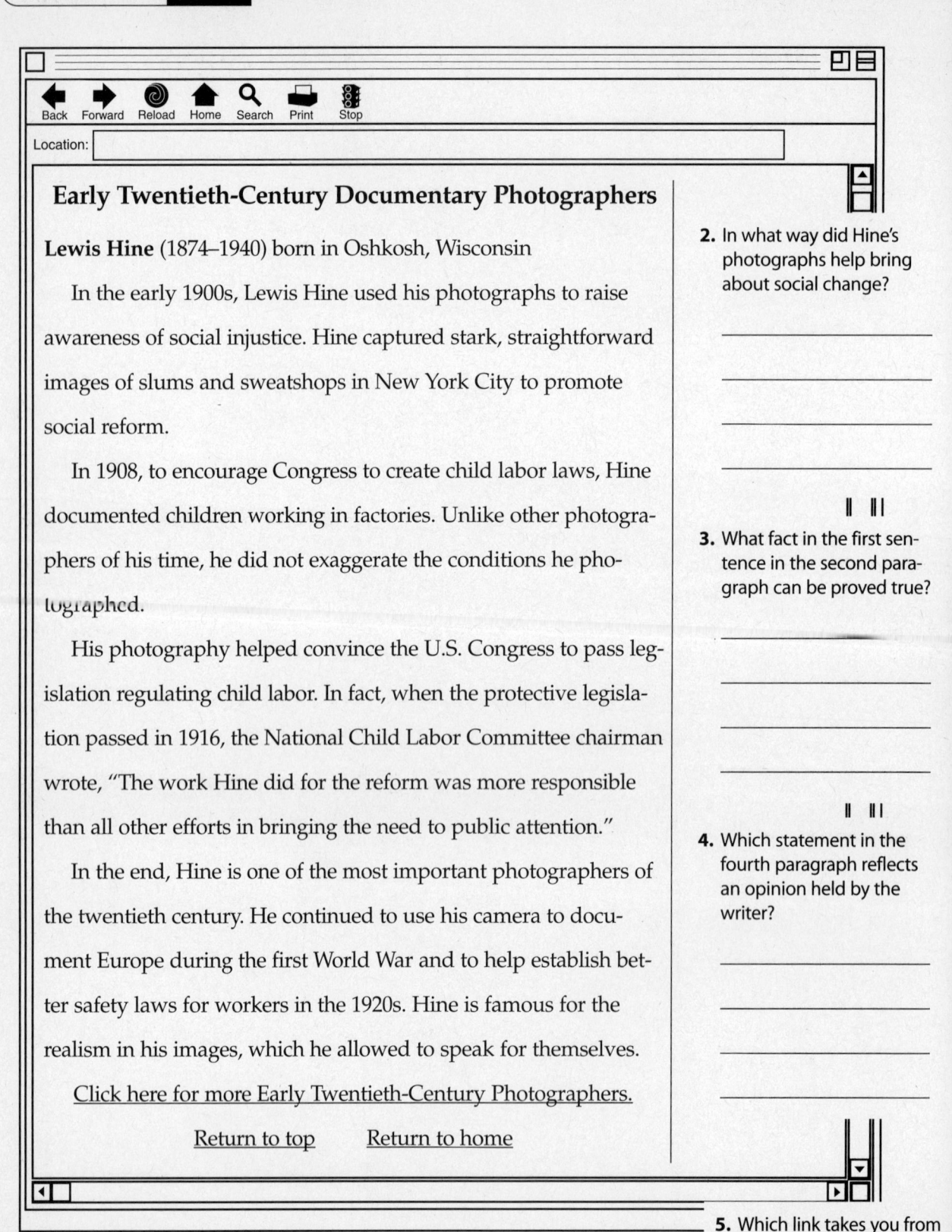

Early Twentieth-Century Documentary Photographers

Lewis Hine (1874–1940) born in Oshkosh, Wisconsin

In the early 1900s, Lewis Hine used his photographs to raise awareness of social injustice. Hine captured stark, straightforward images of slums and sweatshops in New York City to promote social reform.

In 1908, to encourage Congress to create child labor laws, Hine documented children working in factories. Unlike other photographers of his time, he did not exaggerate the conditions he photographed.

His photography helped convince the U.S. Congress to pass legislation regulating child labor. In fact, when the protective legislation passed in 1916, the National Child Labor Committee chairman wrote, "The work Hine did for the reform was more responsible than all other efforts in bringing the need to public attention."

In the end, Hine is one of the most important photographers of the twentieth century. He continued to use his camera to document Europe during the first World War and to help establish better safety laws for workers in the 1920s. Hine is famous for the realism in his images, which he allowed to speak for themselves.

Click here for more Early Twentieth-Century Photographers.

Return to top   Return to home

---

2. In what way did Hine's photographs help bring about social change?

3. What fact in the first sentence in the second paragraph can be proved true?

4. Which statement in the fourth paragraph reflects an opinion held by the writer?

5. Which link takes you from this page back to the site's home page?

NAME _____ CLASS _____ DATE _____

for **CHAPTER 5** page 158 continued **TEST**

DIRECTIONS Use the information in the Web site you have just read to complete the flowchart.

Creating a Web Site Flowchart

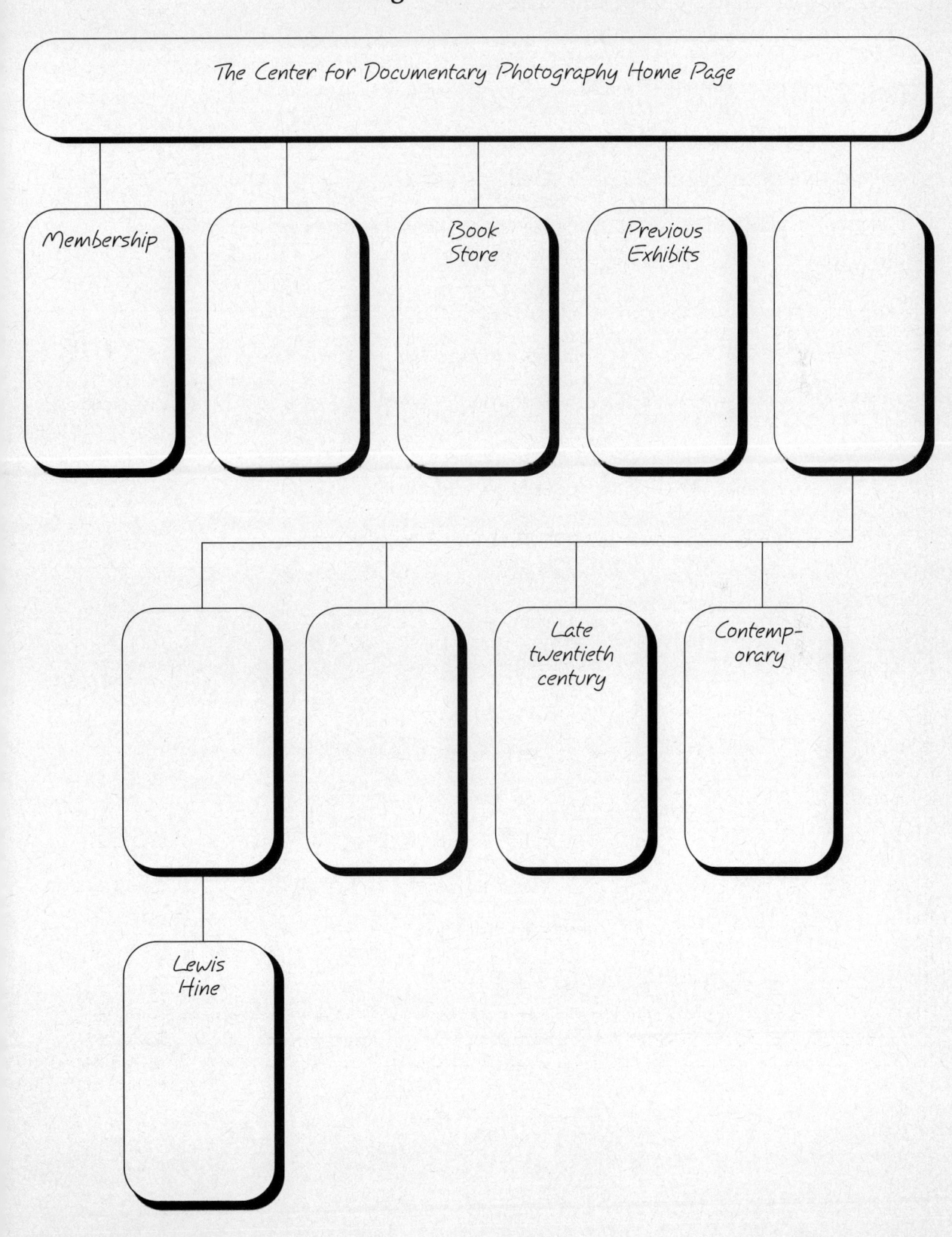

The Center for Documentary Photography Home Page

- Membership
-
- Book Store
- Previous Exhibits
-

-
-
- Late twentieth century
- Contemporary

- Lewis Hine

Chapter Tests

27

for **CHAPTER 5** page 169

REVISING GUIDELINES

Writing Workshop: Research Report

DIRECTIONS Use the following guidelines to help you revise and correct the report on the next page.

THE INTRODUCTION SHOULD
- grab the reader's attention
- contain a clear main idea statement

▼

THE BODY SHOULD
- contain paragraphs that explain only one subject subtopic
- contain paragraphs that include facts, statistics, examples, quotations, or conclusions that elaborate on the subject

▼

CONCLUSION SHOULD
- include an unanswered question or a final comment

▼

THE WORKS CITED LIST SHOULD
- contain at least three sources, which are used in the paper
- contain all sources that are used in the paper

REMEMBER TO
- ❏ revise wordy sentences
- ❏ format sources properly

Writing Workshop: Revising and Proofreading

DIRECTIONS The following report was written in response to this prompt:

Write a cause-and-effect report on a health-related topic.

The report contains problems in style, content, and mechanics.
- Use the space between the lines to revise the paper and correct the errors.
- If you cannot fit some of your revisions between the lines, rewrite the revised sections on a separate piece of paper.

The Comfrey Plant

Long before pharmaceutical companies manufactured medications, people relied upon plants for healing. Even today, the comfrey plant is known for its healing qualities. However, this plant must be used with extreme caution. Comfrey can cause very harmful side effects, especially if taken internally.

The comfrey plant contains several chemicals that, when applied directly to wounds, cause cell production and reduce swelling. These healing properties of this plant, which is known as comfrey, are thought to help restore the skin to its healthy state that it was in before being wounded.

a. Problem with wordiness

To obtain comfrey's benefits, people can place crushed leaves directly on a wound. Comfrey is a good example of why herbs should be regulated. People may also use juice from the leaves to treat the skin (Conrad and Murray 84). The benefits of using comfrey on the skin have not been proven, but comfrey is generally considered safe ("Comfrey" 1).

b. Problem with more than one subtopic in paragraph

However, some herbalists have said that they are concerned due to the fact that comfrey contains powerful toxins that can damage the liver. Dr. Andrew Weil, a popular health expert, thinks that the comfrey root is more harmful than the leaves, but he still does not recommend taking it orally (Weil 1).

c. Problem with wordiness

Although the government does not regulate herb remedies and has not established a safe dosage for comfrey, this plant has a strong reputation for healing. As with any medical treatment, before using this herb, discuss its effects with a doctor you trust.

Works Cited

"Comfrey." *thriveonline*. thrive@health. 13 May 2000 <http://www.thrive.net/health/Library/vitamins/vitamin131.html>.

Conrad, James, and Stephen Murray. Odena's Texas Herb Book. Wolfe City, Texas: Lavender Hill Herb Farm, 1990.

d. Problem with source citation

Weil, Dr. Andrew. "Q & A: Comfort and Caution with Comfrey?" *Ask Dr. Weil*. 4 Aug. 1999. VitaminShoppe.com. 9 May 2000 <http://www.pathfinder.com/drweil/qa_answer/0,3189,1034,00.html>.

NAME _____ CLASS _____ DATE _____ SCORE _____

for **CHAPTER 6** page 204   TEST

Reading Workshop: Persuasive Essay

DIRECTIONS Read the following passage, and answer the questions in the right-hand column.

A Noble Solution

All too often, a sad and avoidable scene repeats itself: a stray pet wanders the streets and finally ends up in an overcrowded shelter. There, the stray might or might not be rescued and given a second chance by a caring owner. Every year, eight to ten million unwanted animals crowd into shelters. There is often not enough room to house all of the animals; of those that end up in shelters, nearly half are put to sleep because there is nowhere else to keep them. There is, however, something you can do to help—adopt a companion animal, rather than buying one from a pet store.

By adopting a pet from an animal shelter, you reduce the supply and demand cycle that keeps pet stores in stock. The demand for pets from large retail chains keeps questionable suppliers called "puppy mills" in business. Over 4,000 of these suppliers operate in the United States. Problems with these businesses frequently include minimal veterinary care, poor quality of food and shelter, overcrowding, and unsanitary and inhumane living conditions for the animals. In addition, because pet stores do not provide a screening process for owners or require altering (spaying or neutering), many pet store animals eventually end up in shelters. By adopting from a shelter instead of buying from a retail store, you can help put an end to this sad cycle.

Adopting a pet offers several benefits to pet owners. One of the biggest advantages to adopting previously owned pets is that they have probably been housebroken. Rescue agencies frequently provide house training. Furthermore, pets from shelters have all their current shots, are heartworm negative, and have already been

---

1. What is the writer's opinion about adopting pets?
_____
_____
_____
_____
_____

2. What purpose do the statistics in the first paragraph serve?
_____
_____
_____
_____
_____

3. In the second paragraph, what reason does the writer give for having his opinion?
_____
_____
_____
_____
_____

Chapter Tests   **31**

altered, saving you money on veterinary care. In addition, most pet adoption agencies provide a careful screening process that helps match owners with suitable pets. Even if owners are looking for a particular breed, they can find what they are looking for; over three million of the dogs in shelters are purebreds.

Adoption from a shelter also gives animals another chance at having a loving home. In many cases, it saves an animal's life. After a period of adjustment, rescued strays tend to bond closely with adoptive families. They can sense they have been brought into a caring household and no longer have to suffer life on the streets. The caring atmosphere of a good home helps them overcome the trauma of having been lost, abandoned, or mistreated.

Those willing to adopt a pet will find a wide variety of kittens, puppies, adults, mixed breeds, and purebreds to choose from. For the cost of a small donation to the shelter, you can take home a companion animal that is housebroken, current on its shots, and a perfect match for you and your family. In addition, you are probably saving a life. Adopting a pet is a great way to help improve the lives of unwanted strays, one animal at a time.

4. In the third paragraph, what is one piece of evidence the writer gives to show that adopting a pet benefits owners?

_____
_____
_____
_____
_____

5. Is the appeal in the fourth paragraph more logical or more emotional? How can you tell?

_____
_____
_____
_____
_____
_____
_____

NAME _____ CLASS _____ DATE _____

for CHAPTER 6 page 204 continued

TEST

DIRECTIONS Use the ideas and information in the passage you have just read to complete the graphic organizer.

Identifying Logical Appeals

TYPE OF EVIDENCE   **EXAMPLES**

FACTS:
- Problems with these businesses frequently include minimal veterinary care, poor quality of food and shelter, overcrowding, and unsanitary and inhumane living conditions.
- _____
- _____
- _____

STATISTICS:
- _____
- _____
- _____

_____:
- A stray pet wanders the streets and finally ends up in an overcrowded shelter.

Chapter Tests

33

NAME _____ CLASS _____ DATE _____

for **CHAPTER 6** page 212

REVISING GUIDELINES

Writing Workshop: Persuasive Essay

DIRECTIONS Use the following guidelines to help you revise and correct the essay on the next page.

THE INTRODUCTION SHOULD
- include an attention-grabbing beginning
- include a clear opinion statement

THE BODY SHOULD
- include logical support (reasons) for the opinion statement
- support each reason with at least one piece of evidence
- include elaboration to clarify reasons or evidence
- present reasons in order of logical importance

THE CONCLUSION SHOULD
- restate the writer's opinion
- summarize the reasons for the writer's opinion
- include a call to action or closing statement

REMEMBER TO
- ❏ vary sentence beginnings
- ❏ avoid delayed or lost subjects

34   ELEMENTS OF LANGUAGE | Second Course

NAME _____ CLASS _____ DATE _____ SCORE _____

for **CHAPTER 6** page 212

TEST

Writing Workshop: Revising and Proofreading

DIRECTIONS The following persuasive essay was written in response to this prompt:

> **Identify something in your neighborhood that you believe could be improved. Persuade others in your area to become involved.**

The essay contains problems in content, style, and usage.

- Choose from the information in the **Databank** on the next page to help you with the revisions.
- Use the space between the lines to revise the paper and correct the errors.
- If you cannot fit your revisions between the lines, rewrite the revised sections on a separate piece of paper.

Create a Neighborhood Wildscape

Do you want to help make our neighborhood a better place while getting outside and having fun? Do you think you have to go a long way out of our neighborhood to enjoy nature? Many people in our community think so. Our part of town lacks green spaces. Unfortunately, you might feel that the solution to this problem is out of your hands or that it is too difficult or expensive to fix. One step in the right direction would be to replace the vacant lot on Fourth and Jenkins with a wildscape. Making a wildscape out of the vacant lot offers us an easy solution that is good for our community and the environment.

It is believed that it is easy to get rid of a neighborhood eyesore. All we need to do to make that unattractive space beautiful again is ask the city to stop mowing it. Then, simply plant native plants, trees, and shrubs, and let them grow on their own. Afterwards, the native plants reseed themselves naturally. Nothing could be simpler.

a. Problem with "it is" construction

Chapter Tests

35

Planting a wildscape in the lot can help our community in several ways. We will make our neighborhood more beautiful. We will also feel more like a group and have a good reason to get together by working on this project. Then, when we work together to get the seeds and starters for native plants, trees, and shrubs, we'll learn a lot about natural plant species and our local environment. In addition, once we start working on one vacant lot, other residents may be inspired to begin making small improvements to other lots.

b. Problem with sentence beginnings

Adding a wildscape in our neighborhood is good for the environment. First of all, a wildscape helps cut back on pollution. Putting a wildscape in the lot will also attract a variety of plant and animal species. One wildscape that neighbors created in White Rock Lake, Texas, attracts birds and butterflies and supports rare native plants.

c. Problem with evidence

Anyone in our community can participate in creating the wildscape. The small amount of effort we put into this simple project can help our neighborhood and local environment in many ways.

d. Problem with call to action

DATABANK
- Combustion-engine lawn mowers use more gasoline and emit more pollutants than cars do.
- Talking to neighbors about this issue is a good way to get them to help.
- Sasha Tsinman at the local department of parks is in charge of signing up volunteers.

NAME _____ CLASS _____ DATE _____ SCORE _____

for **CHAPTER 7** page 240

TEST

Reading Workshop: Brochure

DIRECTIONS Read the following brochure, and answer the questions in the right-hand column.

Front Panel

Hillcrest Riding Center

where excellence is part of the course

1. Do you think that an illustration is an effective medium for this brochure? Why?

_____
_____
_____
_____
_____

2. What story does the picture suggest? How does it encourage people to read further?

_____
_____
_____
_____
_____

3. Are the words in the slogan positive or negative?

_____
_____
_____
_____

Chapter Tests

Inside Spread

Become a part of the tradition.

For thirty-five years, Hillcrest Riding Center has attracted both beginning riders and professional horse trainers. Owner Tom McGown, a licensed jockey, rode such thoroughbred greats as Silver Boy and High Spirits to victory.

Now retired from racing, Tom and his staff provide riding instruction as well as superior boarding care.

Facilities include

- lighted outdoor arena for night riding
- indoor arena for rainy weather
- boarding stable
- stadium obstacle course
- cross-country obstacle course
- on-site tack shop
- designated grooming areas

4. What information in the inside spread helps support the slogan "Become a part of the tradition"?

5. What kind of photo would draw you in and make you more interested in the facilities—a photo made up of cool colors or a photo made up of warm colors? Explain your answer.

Inside Spread Continued

Ride with champions.

Hillcrest has an excellent stable of quality school horses. Newly retired racehorses challenge the advanced rider while our more seasoned horses please the beginner. Hillcrest stands apart from stables that offer untrained or aging horses.

You are also welcome to board your own champion in our secure boarding stable.

Whether you bring your own horse or use ours, you will have the opportunity to learn

- care and grooming of the horse
- basic horsemanship
- jumping

Achieve your personal best.

- Gain confidence and poise.
- Build strength and energy.
- Learn at your own level.
- Attain your personal best.

6. Based on the slogan "Ride with champions," what do you think is the writer's point of view? Explain your answer.

7. Why does the writer repeat the words *personal best*?

NAME _____ CLASS _____ DATE _____

for **CHAPTER 7** page 240 continued

TEST

Back Panel

Hillcrest Riding Center

The center is located at the junction of Highway 378 and County Road 39. For a personal tour of our facility, contact Beverly at 555-3763. Hours are 8:00 A.M. to 4:00 P.M., Monday through Saturday.

Saddle Up with Us

Private lessons: $35 for one hour

Group lessons: $25 for one hour

The price of a lesson includes the use of our saddles and tack.

Full-care boarding: $375 per month

Self-care boarding: $250 per month

Full-care boarding includes feed, shavings, daily turnout, grooming, and maintenance veterinary care. Self-care boarding includes feed only.

We use the services of equine specialist Stanley Hall, D.V.M., for veterinary care.

8. Why is this last statement included?

_____
_____
_____
_____
_____

for **CHAPTER 7** page 240 continued

TEST

DIRECTIONS Use the details from the brochure text below to complete the following.

Identifying Point of View

Text:

For thirty-five years, Hillcrest Riding Center has attracted both beginning riders and professional horse trainers. Owner Tom McGown, a licensed jockey, rode such thoroughbred greats as Silver Boy and High Spirits to victory.

Now retired from racing, Tom and his staff provide riding instruction as well as superior boarding care.

Hillcrest has an excellent stable of quality school horses. Newly retired racehorses challenge the advanced rider while our more seasoned horses please the beginner. Hillcrest stands apart from stables that offer untrained or aging horses.

Positive words:

_____

_____

Negative words:

_____

_____

Patterns in words: _All the positive words describe Hillcrest. The negative words describe the competition._

_____

_____

Writer's point of view:

_____

_____

NAME _____ CLASS _____ DATE _____

for CHAPTER 7 page 250   **REVISING GUIDELINES**

Writing Workshop: Brochure

DIRECTIONS Use the following guidelines to help you revise and correct the brochure on the next page.

THE BROCHURE COPY SHOULD
- name the product or service on the front panel
- contain a short, catchy, and memorable slogan
- give convincing reasons and clear details that explain how the reader will benefit from the product or service
- provide key information that tells everything the reader needs to know about the product or service
- include a clear call to action on the back panel

▼

THE ILLUSTRATIONS SHOULD
- explain important details and make readers want to read the text

REMEMBER TO
- ❑ include words that have a strong emotional impact
- ❑ use commas correctly between adjectives

42   ELEMENTS OF LANGUAGE | Second Course

NAME _____ CLASS _____ DATE _____ SCORE _____

for **CHAPTER 7** page 250   **TEST**

Writing Workshop: Revising and Proofreading

DIRECTIONS The following brochure was written in response to this prompt:

   Create a brochure for a product or a service.

This brochure contains problems in content, style, punctuation, and usage.

- Use the space between the lines to revise the brochure and correct the errors.
- If you cannot fit some of your revisions between the lines, rewrite the revised sections on a separate piece of paper.

Front Panel

Zack and Willie's

We fix stuff for you.

a. Problem with information

b. Problem with slogan

Chapter Tests   **43**

Inside Spread

What we do

Parents, are you tired of waiting at the computer service area in the big stores? Are you tired of that flat empty wallet or those tedious long credit card statements?

Take the worry and expense out of your computer troubles. Let Zack and Willie handle them for you.

- We repair and service all brands of PCs.

- We'll give you credit for your old computer and parts and apply that credit toward new parts, service, or a new computer that we build just for you.

- We'll make sure your computer is up and running in time for you to play computer games after school.

c. Problem with punctuation

d. Problem with reason

Inside Spread, continued

Trust us.
Our parents do.

Zack's dad has been a computer programmer at a major electronics company for seventeen years. He taught Zack how to work on computers and even lets him fix the family's personal computer.

Willie uses new, accurate, professional, electronic tools and equipment for repairs.

e. Problem with punctuation

- Most people don't know that dust and cobwebs are a PC's worst enemy. We specialize in cleaning PCs.

- We can also tell if lightning has hurt your computer.

f. Problem with emotional language

- We care and do a nice job.

Back Panel

Zack and Willie's
Computer Repair and Rebuilding Fact Sheet

Where: We fix them in Willie's house.

When: Anytime between 5:00 P.M. and 9:00 P.M.

Cost: $15 per hour

1 hour minimum/10 hour maximum

Tell us all about your PC woes

at 522-1000

We trade old PC parts for new!

g. Problem with key information

Writing Effective Sentences

CHAPTER TEST

REVISING FRAGMENTS AND RUN-ON SENTENCES

DIRECTIONS Decide whether the following word groups are fragments or run-ons. Then, revise each word group to make it clear and complete. Remember to add correct capitalization and punctuation.

Example After they won the game. ~~The~~ , the team celebrated.

1. The hunter at the snake when he heard its rattle.

2. Leonardo da Vinci was an important Renaissance artist, his drawings reveal that he was also interested in science.

3. Even though the fire had gone out.

4. Was towed away because it had been parked in a fire lane.

5. It snowed last Tuesday we went skiing.

COMBINING SENTENCES

DIRECTIONS Combine the following sentence groups to make one clear and complete sentence. Remember to add correct capitalization and punctuation. Use the headings above each set of sentences to guide you.

Example Today the term *Renaissance person* is applied to gifted individuals. ~~The people~~ who are interested in many fields.

Inserting Words

6. George Washington believed in developing the western United States. His belief was strong.

Inserting Phrases

7. George Washington rejected the idea of kingship. He later became the first president of the United States.

8. Sammy Sosa started playing major league baseball with the Texas Rangers. He started playing major league baseball in 1989.

9. Next week, Katy's uncle will visit. He is a fisherman.

Forming Compound Subjects and Verbs

10. Manatees live in Florida's Everglades. Panthers live in Florida's Everglades.

11. Maria visited the museum with her French class. She bought a postcard of the *Mona Lisa*.

Forming Compound Sentences

12. Lena loves Mexican food. She does not order dishes that are too hot and spicy.

13. The circus came to town. All of my friends bought tickets.

Using Subordinate Clauses to Combine Sentences

14. Michelangelo was a Renaissance artist. He is famous for painting the Sistine Chapel.

15. The students ate at an outdoor café. They could watch the boats on the James River.

IMPROVING SENTENCE STYLE

DIRECTIONS The following sentences are stringy or wordy. Revise each one to improve sentence style. Remember to use correct capitalization and punctuation.

Example We went to the store ~~and then we went~~ to the movies and ~~then we went~~ to a restaurant.

16. We had to cancel the picnic due to the fact that it rained.

17. The amusement park had two roller coasters and one was called The Skyscraper and the other was called The Widow Maker.

18. When the mail carrier delivered the package, Vanessa had to sign a receipt that showed that she had received what she had been sent.

19. Lester invited us to his computer party and we played video games and we ate spaghetti.

20. Some people travel to Nags Head, North Carolina to sun on the beach and other people go there to go deep-sea fishing.

REVISING A PASSAGE

DIRECTIONS The following passage contains sentences that need to be improved. Using what you have learned, revise the underlined portions. Make your corrections in the space between the lines.

Look for
- sentence fragments
- run-on sentences
- stringy sentences

Example   Colonel Guion Bluford, Jr. studied hard, ~~He~~ became an astronaut.

and

Guion Bluford, Jr., the First African American Astronaut

(21) <u>African Americans have made important contributions to America's space program, the first African American to travel in space was Colonel Guion S. Bluford, Jr.</u> **(22)** <u>Colonel Bluford a crew member of the space shuttle *Challenger*.</u> He participated in the first night launch of a space shuttle.

Colonel Bluford was born on November 22, 1942, in Philadelphia, Pennsylvania. **(23)** <u>As a young boy, he read about airplanes. And built models of them.</u> In school, he was interested in aeronautical engineering. **(24)** <u>The school counselor discouraged Bluford's interest in aerospace and told him to go into auto mechanics and he also told him to try carpentry.</u>

Colonel Bluford was determined to pursue his childhood dream. He earned his Ph.D. in aerospace engineering at Penn State University and became a mission specialist for NASA in 1970. **(25)** <u>Conducted scientific experiments while on board spacecraft.</u> When the space shuttle *Challenger* lifted off on August 30, 1983, Colonel Bluford's dream came true.

for CHAPTER 9 page 294

Learning About Paragraphs

CHAPTER TEST

DIRECTIONS Read the two paragraphs below and the passage on the next page. Then, use what you have learned about the parts of a paragraph to answer the items in the right column.

EXAMPLE

Last Friday, our class went on a field trip to the science museum. As a result, I learned a great deal about aircraft and spacecraft. Consequently, I entered my project in the school's science fair.

1. Write the transition words or phrases used in the paragraph above.

   As a result

   consequently

Paragraph 1

Like *shark,* the word *piranha* may strike terror in the hearts of people. Piranhas, native to South America, are related to minnows and catfish. However, unlike minnows and catfish, piranhas have strong jaws and razor-sharp teeth. Piranhas may grow as long as two feet and may attack in schools of over a thousand. Attracted by the smell of blood, these carnivorous fish have been known to devour a one-hundred-pound mammal in less than a minute.

clincher sentence:_____

_____

Paragraph 2

I will never forget my first school dance. The ordinary school gym had been transformed into a wonderland. The scruffy wooden gym floor was sanded and polished so that I could see my face in it. Today, the gym is often used for night games on Tuesdays and Thursdays. Red and blue balloons floated along the high ceiling while golden streamers adorned the stage. The boys, dressed in their finest clothes, huddled shyly in one corner of the gym; and the girls, in their prettiest dresses, stood at the far end, giggling. From the stage, two giant speakers boomed a popular song. I walked toward one of the girls and mustered all the courage I could manage: "May I have this dance?"

1. Underline the topic sentence of Paragraph 1.

2. Write a clincher sentence to conclude Paragraph 1.

3. Write the main idea of Paragraph 2.

   _____
   _____
   _____

4. Cross out the sentence that destroys the unity of Paragraph 2.

5. Use sensory details to write a sentence that will fit into Paragraph 2 and support the main idea.

   _____
   _____
   _____

50   ELEMENTS OF LANGUAGE | Second Course

Deadly Storms

Every year tornadoes rip through the countryside and hurricanes attack the coast, taking people's lives and damaging entire communities. Tornadoes and hurricanes may well be two of the most destructive forces on Earth.

Both tornadoes and hurricanes are types of cyclones, air masses that spin around an area of low pressure. Tornadoes stem from thunderclouds that occur over land. Tornadoes most commonly form in the heart of the United States. Texas, Oklahoma, and Kansas are part of a region known as Tornado Alley because so many tornadoes occur there. Hurricanes, on the other hand, form at sea. They take shape in the Atlantic Ocean and most commonly affect the Caribbean. Hurricanes can sweep the eastern seaboard from Florida to New England.

Tornadoes reach higher wind speeds than hurricanes. A tornado's winds range from forty miles per hour to nearly three hundred miles per hour, while hurricane winds range from seventy-three miles per hour to about two hundred miles per hour. Meteorologists record several tornadoes each year with speeds close to three hundred miles per hour. Two factors make hurricanes more destructive than tornadoes: the difference in the size of each storm and the length of time each storm can last. Tornadoes are smaller in size and shorter in duration than hurricanes. A tornado seldom becomes larger than .25 miles in diameter, although the diameter can range from twenty feet to one mile. It travels an average of seven to eight miles before dissipating. A hurricane, however, can extend more than five hundred miles in diameter and can affect thousands of square miles and millions of people. While tornadoes usually do not last longer than a few minutes, a hurricane may last weeks, causing flooding, torrential rainfall, and billions of dollars in property damage. A tornado warning, the period when a tornado has been seen or is highly likely, generally lasts only forty-five minutes.

Even though a hurricane can cause more damage than a tornado, both are deadly, violent storms. Hurricanes and tornadoes destroy lives and property and demand our respect.

---

6. What type of order is used in the second paragraph—chronological, spatial, order of importance, or logical?

7. Use the paragraph symbol (¶) to show where a new paragraph should begin.

8. Write a topic sentence for the third paragraph.

9. Circle the sentence that is out of order in the new fourth paragraph, and draw an arrow showing where it belongs.

10. Write three transitional words or phrases that appear in this passage.

Pasta: Who Cooked It Up?

For centuries, pasta has been a staple food around the world. Even though no one knows who first created pasta, several theories exist.

Legend has it that the Italian explorer Marco Polo discovered pasta in China and other Asian countries in 1292 and brought it to Italy. It is true that the Chinese had been making a noodle-like food since 3000 B.C. Polo also discovered that the Chinese had developed gunpowder. However, people have eaten pasta in Italy since the time of the Roman Republic: The Roman writer Cicero mentions his fondness for a pasta made of ribbons of boiled dough similar to spaghetti. People in Rome were eating ravioli in the late 1200s, when Marco Polo was a boy. Other people claim that pasta originated in the Middle East, where Egyptian hieroglyphics dating to the fourth century B.C. show a group of Egyptians making what appears to be pasta. Arab travelers made a dry form of pasta from flour and water. They stored it for long periods of time and cooked it quickly in boiling water while traveling in the desert.

While the origin of pasta is a mystery, its use seems almost universal. Greek mythology may even contain a reference: The god Vulcan created a device that could make strings of dough. Could he have been making spaghetti? No matter where it was first cooked and eaten, however, pasta will continue to be a favorite around the globe.

11. Underline the topic sentence of the second paragraph.

12. Cross out the sentence that destroys the unity of the second paragraph.

13. Use the paragraph symbol (¶) to show where a new paragraph should begin.

14. Circle the word that shows transition in the second paragraph.

15. Are the paragraphs in this passage narrative, expository, descriptive, or persuasive?

NAME	CLASS	DATE	SCORE

for CHAPTER 10 page 322   **CHAPTER TEST**

The Sentence: Subject and Predicate, Kinds of Sentences

A. IDENTIFYING SENTENCES AND SENTENCE FRAGMENTS Identify each of the following groups of words as a sentence or a sentence fragment. On the line provided, write *S* for *sentence* or *F* for *fragment*.

Examples __*F*__ 1. After attending the film festival.

            __*S*__ 2. The film festival begins Monday.

_____ 1. Highly creative movies are shown at the festival each year.

_____ 2. Want to see as many of them as possible.

_____ 3. Does the newspaper list a schedule of the movies?

_____ 4. When the animated movies are shown during the weekend.

_____ 5. Filmmakers from all over the world send their best films for the event.

_____ 6. From as far as India and China, for example, and from as close as our neighbors, Canada and Mexico.

_____ 7. How young filmmakers can get valuable publicity and become better known.

_____ 8. Buy tickets early!

_____ 9. Sometimes movie stars attend the festival.

_____ 10. Watching so many films in a few days.

B. IDENTIFYING COMPLETE SUBJECTS AND SIMPLE SUBJECTS In each of the following sentences, underline the complete subject once and the simple subject twice. (Reminder: A simple subject may be compound.)

Example 1. Making large vapor trails in the sky were two jets.

11. Everyone in our class wants to go on the trip.

12. When will the bus arrive to pick up the band members?

13. In less than two weeks, the industrious beavers dammed the stream.

14. Holding the newborn baby was the proud father.

15. Will Gretchen or Aaron take turns using the computer?

16. Do all those television ads feature talking pandas?

17. Shawn, Lynn, and Willa have weekend jobs.

18. Fresh mozzarella cheese and tomatoes make up her favorite Italian salad.

19. How well you sing!

20. Tomorrow the new lights on the corner by our house will be installed.

Chapter Tests   **53**

NAME _____ CLASS _____ DATE _____ SCORE _____

for **CHAPTER 10** page 322 continued   **CHAPTER TEST**

C. IDENTIFYING COMPLETE PREDICATES AND SIMPLE PREDICATES In each of the following sentences, underline the complete predicate once and the simple predicate twice. (Reminder: A simple predicate may be compound.)

Example 1. In an art book I <u>read about Ch'i Pai-shih and saw some of his work.</u>

21. He was truly an amazing and talented artist.
22. He also is known as Ch'i Huang.
23. Ch'i Pai-shih has been called China's Picasso.
24. Didn't he paint and carve and do calligraphy?
25. Common subjects such as birds and flowers appealed to him.
26. How some people objected to his subjects and art!
27. The roots of his art are firmly set in Chinese folk traditions.
28. When did he begin his career?
29. At the age of twenty-seven, Ch'i Pai-shih first studied art.
30. As a youth he worked as a carpenter and a woodcarver.

D. IDENTIFYING SUBJECTS AND VERBS In each of the following sentences, underline the simple subject once and the verb or verb phrase twice. (Reminder: A subject, a verb, or both may be compound.)

Example 1. In the <u>refrigerator</u> <u>is</u> a special <u>treat</u> for you.

31. The bike against the fence belongs to my cousin.
32. Why did you get so many telephone calls last night?
33. On their fourth trip to St. Louis, my mother and father finally went to the top of the Gateway Arch.
34. Are cars and trucks allowed in this part of the park?
35. At the top of the tallest pine tree sits a young bald eagle.
36. When will you return, Aunt Ruthie?
37. The judge originally agreed but later changed his mind.
38. Under the watchful eye of their grandmother, Karen and Mary Beth played and bounced on the trampoline.
39. Joking and acting silly through dinner were Ron's guests.
40. After the storm, the National Guard helped the repair crews.

54   ELEMENTS OF LANGUAGE | Second Course

NAME _____ CLASS _____ DATE _____ SCORE _____

for **CHAPTER 10** page 322 continued **CHAPTER TEST**

E. CLASSIFYING AND PUNCTUATING SENTENCES Classify each of the following sentences by writing *DEC* for *declarative*, *IMP* for *imperative*, *INT* for *interrogative*, or *EXC* for *exclamatory* on the line provided. Add the correct end punctuation to each sentence.

Example _IMP_ 1. Quick, catch him!

_____ 41. What a great concert that was last night

_____ 42. When did Jorge's uncle arrive from Argentina

_____ 43. The longest day of the year is tomorrow

_____ 44. Please close the door when you leave

_____ 45. Will the historic building be preserved

_____ 46. Stop the car

_____ 47. My address book now contains thirty-nine e-mail addresses

_____ 48. Help me remember his name

_____ 49. How pure is your city's drinking water

_____ 50. Joshua asked to use the electric drill

Chapter Tests **55**

| NAME | CLASS | DATE | SCORE |

for CHAPTER 11 *page 344*   **CHAPTER TEST**

Parts of Speech Overview: Noun, Pronoun, Adjective

A. IDENTIFYING TYPES OF NOUNS In each of the following sentences, underline each noun that is the type indicated in parentheses. (Reminder: There may be more than one type of noun in a sentence.)

Example 1. Some people have expressed <u>concern</u> and <u>regret</u> that traditional ceremonies in Africa seem to be disappearing. *(abstract)*

1. African countries such as Ethiopia, Namibia, and Morocco each have distinctive ceremonies. *(proper)*

2. Do you have much knowledge about rituals and ceremonies of African peoples? *(abstract)*

3. Carol Beckwith and Angela Fisher spent years doing fieldwork to create a photographic record of vanishing rituals in Africa. *(compound)*

4. Sue's grandmother loaned me a copy of their book, titled *African Ceremonies*. *(compound)*

5. One photograph shows Yoruba dancers wearing masks and whirling panels in a traditional celebration. *(concrete)*

6. The two photographers had the great honor of receiving permission to witness various ceremonies. *(abstract)*

7. One of the faculty brought in her collection of traditional clothes made of beautiful *kente* cloth. *(collective)*

8. However, modern clothes and accessories are being worn more and more at special events. *(common)*

9. Still, many of the old ways survive; for example, Surma men and women may decorate their faces with chalk during courtship. *(concrete)*

10. I would like to see a festival that celebrates the change of seasons. *(common)*

B. IDENTIFYING TYPES OF PRONOUNS In each of the following sentences, underline the pronoun that is the type indicated in parentheses. (Reminder: There may be more than one type of pronoun in a sentence.)

Example 1. <u>Many</u> of his clients regularly order <u>something</u> every month. *(indefinite)*

11. My uncle, who lives in Taiwan, is a businessman. *(relative)*

12. Arnold himself paid for the refreshments for everyone at the meeting. *(intensive)*

13. "Everything happens for the best" is a favorite saying of many people. *(indefinite)*

14. I have a cap just like that one. *(personal)*

56   ELEMENTS OF LANGUAGE | Second Course

for CHAPTER 11 page 344 *continued*   **CHAPTER TEST**

15. Who do you think will be the next singing sensation? *(interrogative)*

16. Who said that and when? *(demonstrative)*

17. Trish and her friends think of themselves as role models for their younger sisters. *(reflexive)*

18. Those are the two cards that I need to complete this set, which is only part of my collection. *(relative)*

19. What probably will be the top export from Brazil this year? *(interrogative)*

20. All of us players try to help each other. *(indefinite)*

C. IDENTIFYING ADJECTIVES In the following sentences, underline each adjective, and draw an arrow to the word it modifies. Do not include the articles *a*, *an*, or *the*. (Reminder: A sentence may have more than one adjective.)

Example 1. This ship is part of a Norwegian line.

21. From the top deck, we watched the brilliant sunrise over the water.

22. The enormous ship slowly sailed among the Greek islands.

23. Each day of the cruise brought us new surprises.

24. For thirty days we saw beautiful scenery and many wonders.

25. These ships certainly serve an abundant variety of delicious food.

26. The rocky islands looked tiny as we approached them.

27. The Australian captain said that his favorite island is Mykonos.

28. Playful dolphins and curious gulls were among animal sightings.

29. Those creatures were seen every day of the trip.

30. In most ports we did some sightseeing and shopped in local markets.

D. IDENTIFYING NOUNS, PRONOUNS, AND ADJECTIVES Each of the following sentences contains an italicized word or group of words. Identify the part of speech of each italicized word or word group by writing above it *N* for *noun*, *P* for *pronoun*, or *A* for *adjective*.

Example 1. What is the first sound *that* you usually hear in the morning? [P]

31. *Oriental* rugs come in several different sizes and are very popular.

32. "Please state *your* ideas clearly and logically," Mrs. Cohen said.

33. Are you going to *Santa Cruz* in California or in Bolivia?

34. The race track, *which* closed last year, was a mile outside the city limits.

35. Terence's grandmother gave *those* irises to the botanical garden.

Chapter Tests   **57**

for CHAPTER 11 page 344 continued **CHAPTER TEST**

36. Thirsty students were upset when they discovered that the *drinking fountain* was broken.

37. Those berries are poisonous, but *these* aren't.

38. Included among the world's leading religions is *Islam*.

39. I hope *someone* listened to the homework instructions better than I did.

40. Some *movie* posters don't accurately capture the film's story and mood.

41. My brother and I ate *all* of the grapes.

42. In many states the races for seats in the *United States Senate* were extremely close.

43. Isn't that a *Whitney Houston* song they are playing?

44. That was the first bell, so I am not *tardy*.

45. The *excited* waiter brought us two baskets of warm bread.

46. The three deer saved *themselves* by leaping into the lake to escape the fire.

47. Carlos wanted *both* jobs but had time for only one.

48. *What* do you think makes these Italian breadsticks so good?

49. The pitch of *kettledrums*, which are used in symphony orchestras, can be changed.

50. The buck turned sharply and then followed the *herd* to safety.

NAME	CLASS	DATE	SCORE

for **CHAPTER 12** *page 370* **CHAPTER TEST**

Parts of Speech Overview: Verb, Adverb, Preposition, Conjunction, Interjection

A. IDENTIFYING VERBS AND VERB PHRASES Underline the verb or verb phrase in each of the following sentences. Then, circle all helping verbs.

Example 1. Next week, we (are) studying communication among Plains Indians.

1. Have you seen pictures of American Indian sign language?
2. Various groups of Plains Indians with different oral languages could communicate with each other in sign language.
3. It was not used for complicated thoughts.
4. Fairly basic ideas were expressed with sign language.
5. A guest speaker in our class will demonstrate some of the different hand movements for Plains Indian sign language.
6. She may teach us the movements for words such as *friend* and *peace*.
7. We must also learn the movements for *buffalo* and *horse*.
8. These animals were very important to the Plains Indians.
9. Mrs. Dover will be leading a workshop on drum signals.
10. The Plains Indians had developed smoke signals for communication, too.

B. IDENTIFYING TYPES OF VERBS Identify the italicized verb or verb phrase in each of the following sentences as a linking verb, a transitive verb, or an intransitive verb. Above the verb or verb phrase, write *LV* for *linking verb*, *TAV* for *transitive action verb*, or *IAV* for *intransitive action verb*.

Example 1. When *did* you *practice*, Freda? *(IAV)*

11. Sondra *rescued* the kitten from the neighbor's roof.
12. The enchiladas *smell* wonderful and are surely ready to eat!
13. The choir *sang* energetically, though slightly off-key.
14. Because of the heavy snowfall, many students *were* late for school.
15. How long *can* you *stay*, Ernest?
16. The Reeds *bought* their airline tickets online for their trip to South Africa.
17. The campers *shivered* after telling scary stories in the dark.
18. The trio *grew* weary after carrying the banners in the parade for an hour.
19. *Has* Ian *seen* the library's new video about the history of lacrosse?
20. *Did*n't Jenny *act* according to the club's rules?

Chapter Tests

for CHAPTER 12 page 370 continued

CHAPTER TEST

C. IDENTIFYING ADVERBS In the following sentences, underline each adverb, and draw an arrow to the word it modifies. (Reminder: A sentence may have more than one adverb.)

Example 1. We rarely picnic here, even though it is rather close to our house.

21. Suddenly the engine started, and the train slowly chugged forward.

22. Accidents happen quite often at this intersection.

23. Oscar has already returned and is waiting patiently.

24. "I most certainly agree with you!" Violet said.

25. Some people are too quick with their criticism of others, my mother frequently says.

26. Where is that new Italian restaurant?

27. The dog jumped so quickly that it made me drop my glass.

28. The Fourth of July is the time we joyously celebrate our freedom.

29. Melanie is very pleased that she is learning Japanese.

30. Randy and Orion again did not hear the coach's command.

D. IDENTIFYING PREPOSITIONS, PREPOSITIONAL PHRASES AND THEIR OBJECTS, CONJUNCTIONS, AND INTERJECTIONS Each of the following sentences contains at least one italicized word. Above each italicized word, identify its part of speech. Use the following abbreviations: *PREP* for *preposition*, *CONJ* for *conjunction*, *INT* for *interjection*. If the italicized word is a preposition, underline the prepositional phrase, and circle the object of the preposition.

Example 1. Have you ever done any volunteer work *at* your school?

31. *Oh*, there are many opportunities and jobs for eager volunteers.

32. Some people think about helping *but* never do it.

33. *During* the winter, offers to shovel snow are appreciated.

34. Running errands during the weekends *or* after school is helpful.

35. *Wow*! I feel good about my volunteer work.

36. Teachers sometimes welcome assistance *not only* during school *but also* before or after classes.

37. *In addition to* your help in the classroom, you also could volunteer for jobs in the library.

38. In fact, volunteers are probably needed for all sorts of jobs *around* your school.

39. You will likely find that other students, *along with* yourself, recognize the rewards of doing volunteer work.

40. Part of the fun of volunteering is making new friends *and* working together with them.

E. IDENTIFYING PARTS OF SPEECH Identify the part of speech of the italicized word or word group in the following sentences. Write the part of speech above the italicized word or words. Use the following abbreviations: *ADJ* for *adjective*, *ADV* for *adverb*, *N* for *noun*, *V* for *verb*, *PRON* for *pronoun*, *PREP* for *preposition*, *CONJ* for *conjunction*, *INT* for *interjection*.

Example 1. The *jump* was not difficult for the young athlete. [N]

41. What is *that* strange noise?

42. *That* is an interesting cloud shape.

43. "Go *below* and get some supper," the submarine commander ordered.

44. The store's prices are always *below* those of its competitors.

45. The *line* for the Ricky Martin concert circled the building.

46. Please *line* the cupboard shelves with this plaid paper.

47. The new post office is now open *for* business.

48. Though exhausted, the explorers forged ahead, *for* only an hour or so of daylight was left.

49. *My*, this test is difficult!

50. "Let's go to *my* house to call," Ellie said.

NAME _____ CLASS _____ DATE _____ SCORE _____

for **CHAPTER 13** page 398

Complements: Direct and Indirect Objects, Subject Complements

CHAPTER TEST

A. IDENTIFYING SUBJECTS, VERBS, AND COMPLEMENTS In each of the following sentences, underline each subject once, underline each verb twice, and circle each complement. (Reminder: A subject, verb, or complement may be compound.)

Example 1. Dolores sent a (brochure) and newspaper (article) about an exciting festival.

1. I am eager for more information about it.
2. Dolores will send me more details, too.
3. The event is the Hispanic Heritage Festival in Dade County, Miami, Florida.
4. The festival salutes Hispanic traditions and cultures.
5. The organizers each year plan many varied events for the festival.
6. These include educational and sporting activities.
7. Thousands of people attend the October festival.
8. To visitors from northern states, the weather in Miami must seem quite warm for that time of year.
9. My family and I are enthusiastic travelers.
10. The festival could be our next trip!

B. IDENTIFYING DIRECT OBJECTS AND INDIRECT OBJECTS Underline each direct object once and each indirect object twice in each of the following sentences.

Example 1. The jury sent the judge notes at three different times.

11. Did you pick any of the blueberries yourself?
12. Everyone thanked me for a job well done.
13. Sally Ann sent him ten e-mails in one day.
14. The cat surprised both the chipmunk and the blue jay.
15. The class asked the author many questions about her popular book.
16. Who found Mr. Keller's map of the Gold Coast from the 1950s?
17. The director chooses whoever will play Rudolph.
18. For best results, always follow the directions closely.
19. My aunt only sends whoever requests it her special jam.
20. Alvin handed Robin the change from the five-dollar bill.

| NAME | CLASS | DATE | SCORE |

for CHAPTER 13 page 398 *continued* **CHAPTER TEST**

C. IDENTIFYING SUBJECT COMPLEMENTS In the following sentences, underline each subject complement, and identify it as a predicate nominative or a predicate adjective. Above each complement, write *PN* for *predicate nominative* or *PA* for *predicate adjective*. (Reminder: A complement may be compound.)

Example 1. The birthday present that Aunt Jill gave me was *PN* what I truly wanted.

21. My computer has been a useful tool for doing homework and research.
22. The weather turned nasty just as the soccer game began.
23. My favorite actors are they.
24. Senator Ames appears the winner in yesterday's election.
25. How shiny and bright the new car appears in the sunlight!
26. Is the champion whoever stays on the horse the longest?
27. Baklava, a treat from Greece, tastes sweet and is sticky.
28. Travis always stays so quiet during study hall.
29. The local historical museum has been much more successful since remodeling.
30. Alice Walker is both a novelist and a poet.

D. IDENTIFYING COMPLEMENTS Each of the following sentences contains an italicized word or word group that is a complement. Identify each of these italicized complements by writing above it *DO* for *direct object*, *IO* for *indirect object*, *PN* for *predicate nominative*, or *PA* for *predicate adjective*.

Example 1. How *PA beautiful* the sunrise is!

31. Don't some of John's jokes seem awfully *silly*?
32. Our class is studying environmental *hazards*.
33. The samba is a Brazilian *dance* originally from Africa.
34. The rules allowed *us* only ten minutes.
35. Gary ordered two *shirts*, a *pair* of shoes, and a *coat*.
36. The bananas feel *soft* and *squishy*.
37. How *smart* the quiz bowl contestants are!
38. In what year did John F. Kennedy become *President of the United States*?
39. How will the schedule changes affect *whoever has already bought tickets*?
40. Mrs. Ramos has asked *everyone* that she has seen.
41. The most talented member of the choir remains *she*.

Chapter Tests **63**

for CHAPTER 13 page 398 continued   **CHAPTER TEST**

42. The police officer gave the *jaywalker* a warning.

43. Some perfumes smell *horrible*, in my opinion.

44. Mom gave my *sister* and *me* gift certificates.

45. The squirrels stored *acorns* in the tree.

46. The Five Civilized Tribes are the *Cherokee*, *Chickasaw*, *Choctaw*, *Creek*, and *Seminole*.

47. The school has built a new *gymnasium*.

48. Once sickly, the plant now looks *healthy* and *strong*.

49. Henry brought *them* an electric blender to make smoothies for the party.

50. What you see is *what you get*.

NAME _____ CLASS _____ DATE _____ SCORE _____

for **CHAPTER 14** page 414   **CHAPTER TEST**

The Phrase: Prepositional, Verbal, and Appositive Phrases

A. IDENTIFYING AND CLASSIFYING PREPOSITIONAL PHRASES In each of the following sentences, underline each prepositional phrase, and draw an arrow to the word it modifies. Then, classify each prepositional phrase by writing *ADJ* for *adjective phrase* or *ADV* for *adverb phrase* above the phrase.

Example 1. Skyler, our cat <u>from the animal shelter</u> [ADJ], joined our family shortly <u>before our move</u> [ADV].

1. Skyler rode along with us in our minivan.
2. She traveled extremely well for a cat.
3. Skyler always claimed a seat next to the window so that she could watch other animals through the window as we passed them.
4. I made many drawings of her during the trip.
5. She often played among the luggage.
6. A small, brown tabby cat, she was good at hiding.
7. Every so often, she would disappear into her own secret place under the boxes and sacks.
8. Skyler seemed to think that each motel room with its bed, dresser, chairs, and other furniture was our new home.
9. Each morning we searched around the room to find her, and only her favorite cat treats could lure her out of her hiding place.
10. Skyler loves our new home outside Miami near a small bay, which offers her many adventures.

B. IDENTIFYING VERBALS Each of the following sentences contains a verbal (a participle, a gerund, or an infinitive). Underline each verbal. Then, tell what type of verbal it is by writing *PART* for *participle*, *GER* for *gerund*, or *INF* for *infinitive* above the word.

Example 1. In some cases, <u>making</u> [GER] quilts apparently was serious business.

11. The quilts hanging in the exhibit have a special history.
12. The main reason that some African Americans who were slaves made quilts was to communicate Underground Railroad escape plans.
13. Displaying certain quilt patterns communicated the escape plans through a secret code only the slaves knew.
14. Slaves followed the directions indicated by the quilt patterns.
15. Various designs were used to express different messages.
16. For example, fleeing slaves watched for the Monkey Wrench design.

Chapter Tests   **65**

for CHAPTER 14 page 414 continued CHAPTER TEST

17. They knew that design was an alert to gather their tools for an escape.

18. Such designs made sending secret plans easier and safer.

19. *Hidden in Plain View* is a good book to read about the quilts.

20. After viewing the exhibit, I knew much more about the Underground Railroad during the Civil War.

C. IDENTIFYING VERBAL PHRASES Identify the italicized verbal phrases in each of the following sentences by writing *PART* for *participial phrase*, *GER* for *gerund phrase*, or *INF* for *infinitive phrase* above the phrase.

Example 1. The number *to call in an emergency* is 911. [INF]

21. After *listening to the speaker*, Jan had new courage.

22. *To get my sister an autographed photo of Will Smith for her birthday* is our plan.

23. The hail *pelting our house and yard* lasted for almost fifteen minutes.

24. My only chance *to see the coach* is during second period.

25. *Finding the information I needed for my American history report* took more time than I had thought it would.

26. The lion tamers acted quickly *to quiet the big cats*.

27. Mrs. Neal's true love is *riding wooden roller coasters*.

28. This CD, *borrowed from my friend Sergio*, has pop tunes from around the world.

29. Angela likes *fishing for trout in the Adirondacks*.

30. *Looking at himself in the distorted mirror*, Sean laughed.

D. IDENTIFYING APPOSITIVES AND APPOSITIVE PHRASES Underline the appositive or appositive phrase in each of the following sentences.

Example 1. Allen, <u>the best guitarist in the band</u>, is only eighteen years old.

31. Manuel Luis Quezon, first president of the Philippines, was born in 1878.

32. Troy's sister Ellen wrote and directed the original play.

33. The quality of my day depends primarily on one person, me.

34. Mount Everest, the highest peak in the world, is in the Himalayas.

35. The actor, a friend of ours, obviously enjoyed playing the villain.

36. The statesman Draco lived in ancient Greece.

37. Please order me a drink, a small glass of orange juice.

38. Pasta, a favorite meal at our house, is quick and easy to prepare.

39. Mollilu's dog, Spark, was last seen chasing his shadow.

40. Two vehicles, a convertible and a pickup truck, raced past us.

E. IDENTIFYING PHRASES For each of the following sentences, identify the italicized phrase by writing PREP for *prepositional*, PART for *participial*, GER for *gerund*, INF for *infinitive*, or APP for *appositive*.

Example 1. *PART* *Seated in the front row*, we could see perfectly.

41. Have you ever tried that colorful salad, *the one that has beets and walnuts in it*?

42. The chipmunks like *hiding among the rocks on the patio*.

43. *Amused by the joke*, Mr. Ray nevertheless refused to laugh.

44. *In the first chapter*, the ship captain was away on a trip to Honduras.

45. Everyone was ready *to go home after the practice*.

46. *To finish this review* is my goal right now.

47. The donkeys *grazing near the road* belong to the family across the street.

48. Mrs. Devine has lived in the house *next to ours* for fifty-five years.

49. Kudus, *African antelopes*, have long horns.

50. *Owning her own business* has always been Janet's dream.

Chapter Tests

NAME _____ CLASS _____ DATE _____ SCORE _____

for **CHAPTER 15** page 438

CHAPTER TEST

The Clause: Independent and Subordinate Clauses

A. IDENTIFYING INDEPENDENT AND SUBORDINATE CLAUSES For each of the following sentences, identify the clause in italics as independent or subordinate. Above the clause, write *IND* for *independent* or *SUB* for *subordinate*.

Example 1. *SUB*
When Jeff was in Cub Scouts, he rode on a train for the first time.

1. *The trip was short*, but it was very memorable.
2. The friendly man *who took the tickets* was the conductor.
3. Jeff sat by the window; *his friend Myron was beside him*.
4. The boys watched in fascination *as the countryside zoomed by*.
5. The train *that the boys were on* consisted of an engine and seven cars.
6. When another train passed close by theirs, *the boys were startled*.
7. The trip was arranged by the boys' scout leader, *whose father worked for the railroad*.
8. *The train cars were not air-conditioned*, though the windows were open.
9. *Jeff enjoyed the ride*, which was a two-hour round trip up the mountainside and back.
10. *After he grew up*, Jeff rode the train frequently.

B. IDENTIFYING ADJECTIVE CLAUSES Identify the adjective clause in each of the following sentences by underlining it once. Then, circle the relative pronoun or relative adverb in the adjective clause. Finally, underline twice the word or word group to which the pronoun or adverb refers.

Example 1. There is the house (where) I spent my childhood.

11. Most people eagerly look forward to vacations, when they can take a break and relax.
12. The attorney read the case on which the ruling is based.
13. Do you know the cities where the band will play on its tour?
14. The little girl picked the one flower that was growing in the garden.
15. Both programs, which were renewed for next season, are clever.
16. Someone who had been at the football game told Richard the story.
17. The person whose name is chosen wins the diamond earrings.
18. The meteorologists that are on television always seem so cheerful.
19. The woman whom I most admire is Dr. Carolyn Jefferson-Jenkins.
20. Wasn't it she who became the first African American woman to lead the National League of Women Voters?

68 ELEMENTS OF LANGUAGE | Second Course

NAME _____ CLASS _____ DATE _____ SCORE _____

for **CHAPTER 15** page 438 continued **CHAPTER TEST**

C. IDENTIFYING ADVERB CLAUSES Identify the adverb clause in each of the following sentences by underlining it once. Then, circle the subordinating conjunction, and underline twice the word or word group to which it refers.

Example 1. Samuel was <u>treated</u> quickly (when) <u>he was admitted to the emergency clinic</u>.

21. Samuel was taken to the clinic because he had difficulty breathing.
22. He looked as though he was having trouble taking a deep breath.
23. The doctor examined him soon after we got there.
24. Before he began examining Samuel, the doctor asked him and me a lot of questions.
25. As the doctor moved his stethoscope around, he told Samuel to breathe in and out.
26. After the doctor finished, lab technicians conducted a couple of tests.
27. We waited until the test results came back.
28. Since the doctor could not find anything wrong with Samuel's lungs and the tests showed no problem, he released Samuel from the hospital.
29. Because he was not seriously ill, Samuel recovered quickly.
30. Apparently, he had simply pulled a muscle while we were playing basketball.

D. IDENTIFYING NOUN CLAUSES AND THEIR FUNCTIONS In each of the following sentences, identify the noun clause by underlining it once. Then, above the noun clause, tell how the noun clause is used by writing *S* for *subject*, *PN* for *predicate nominative*, *DO* for *direct object*, *IO* for *indirect object*, or *OP* for *object of a preposition*.

IO
Example 1. Please hand <u>whoever has a coupon</u> a free jar of salsa.

31. How the Druids built Stonehenge remains a secret to this day.
32. Did you know that Juan is one of the most popular names given to baby boys born in the United States now?
33. Emma didn't know to whom she should address the letter.
34. Many people in the crowd did not agree with whatever the speaker said.
35. The mother robin gave whichever chick stuck its head up highest the next bit of food.
36. Linda finally told us that we could go swimming.
37. Seven o'clock is when the dance begins.
38. Vietnamese food was what we were craving for dinner.
39. When Marta wants to get her haircut is up to her.
40. Does anyone know why the buses are late this afternoon?

Chapter Tests **69**

E. IDENTIFYING AND CLASSIFYING SUBORDINATE CLAUSES Underline the subordinate clause in each of the following sentences. Then, classify each subordinate clause by writing above it *ADJ* for *adjective clause*, *ADV* for *adverb clause*, or *N* for *noun clause*.

Example 1. Japan is one of the few major world powers <u>that still has a royal family</u>. *ADJ*

41. Akihito, who became emperor of Japan in 1989, does not rule the country.

42. Although Akihito is not the political leader, he plays an important role as ceremonial head of state.

43. Many people have definite ideas about what this ceremonial role should be.

44. Perhaps the chief duty that the emperor must fulfill is to serve as a keeper and role model of Japanese culture.

45. Because he wants to be closer to his people, Akihito speaks modern Japanese and sometimes mixes with the public.

46. That he married a commoner and has raised his own children also displays his dedication to making his position less imperial.

47. While he seeks to lessen the gap between the Imperial family and the Japanese people, Akihito still observes many revered traditions.

48. For example, he officially sits on the Chrysanthemum Throne, which is the ancient seat of Japan's royalty.

49. Also, Akihito and his family maintain much of the lifestyle in which Japan's Imperial family has always lived.

50. Since he became emperor, Akihito has been criticized by modernists as well as traditionalists.

NAME _____ CLASS _____ DATE _____ SCORE _____

for CHAPTER 16 page 458   **CHAPTER TEST**

Sentence Structure: The Four Basic Sentence Structures

A. IDENTIFYING SUBJECTS AND VERBS IN SIMPLE SENTENCES In each of the following simple sentences, underline the subject once and the verb twice. (Reminder: The subjects and verbs may be simple or compound.)

Example 1. Horses, zebras, donkeys, and burros are all equines.

1. Ten-year-old Gabriel loves all members of the equine family.
2. He and his older brother Nathan live with their parents in New Mexico.
3. For his birthday last year, Gabriel received two burros.
4. These were definitely his favorite gifts.
5. Gabriel thought and thought about names for the mother and son burros.
6. Finally, he gave the little brown burro a French name, *Jacques*.
7. Deb, Gabriel's friend, suggested the name *Neige* for the mother burro.
8. *Neige*, the French word for "snow," suits the burro's white coloring.
9. Gabriel and his mother and brother tamed and trained the burros with kindness and food.
10. For fun after school now, Gabriel and Nathan ride and groom Neige and Jacques.

B. IDENTIFYING SUBJECTS, VERBS, AND CONJUNCTIONS IN COMPOUND SENTENCES In each of the following compound sentences, write *S* above each *subject* and *V* above each *verb*. If the clauses in the sentence are joined by a conjunction, write *C* above the conjunction. If the clauses are joined by a conjunctive adverb, write *CA* above the conjunctive adverb.

Example 1. In 1999, Sheila Sisulu was appointed South Africa's first female ambassador to the United States, so she prepared to move to Washington, D.C., to begin her work.

11. Sisulu was born during the first year of formal apartheid in South Africa; as a result, the policy of separation of the races clouded most of her life.

12. From sixth grade on, her hard-working parents sent her to a boarding school in Swaziland; in that British protectorate, she could receive an unprejudiced education.

13. Her brother attended engineering school in the United States, and the South African police harassed the family about his departure.

14. Such actions were aimed at discouraging the black population of South Africa; instead, Sisulu and others fought back against apartheid.

15. In the early days, her qualifications as a teacher were not recognized by the government; consequently, she taught students in an alternative program.

Chapter Tests   **71**

for CHAPTER 16 page 458 continued   CHAPTER TEST

16. Sisulu later earned recognition as an education expert; accordingly, she was appointed to important church and government positions.

17. In Sisulu's opinion, a black South African cannot avoid involvement in politics; in fact, she sees her very existence as a statement of resistance to apartheid.

18. In 1994, she was appointed as Special Advisor to the Minister of Education, and the demands of her new job kept her constantly on the go all over the world.

19. Before becoming ambassador, she worked in New York City as Consul General on U.S.-South Africa relations; therefore, she was accustomed to the United States.

20. Sisulu has never backed down from her beliefs, nor has she settled for less than her dreams for herself and her country.

C. IDENTIFYING INDEPENDENT CLAUSES AND SUBORDINATE CLAUSES IN SENTENCES In each of the following sentences, underline each independent clause once and each subordinate clause twice. (A sentence may have more than one independent clause and more than one subordinate clause.) Above the subject of each clause, write *S*, and above the verb in each clause, write *V*.

Example 1. As soon as the rain began, the tent we had begun to leak, and we ran to the van.

21. Because the weather is unpredictable, the concert will be inside the building.

22. Mrs. Lee is our former neighbor whom we visit when we are in town.

23. After the wedding was over, the groom, who is my cousin, gave each usher a fifty-dollar bill, and of course I got one.

24. When I have time, I hope to read that book that both you and my uncle recommended.

25. If you have time, we can go to the mall and shop for decorations for the party.

26. Since crossword puzzles are time-consuming, I don't work them often, but they are fun to do.

27. Until they were sold, the horses were pastured near our house, and we enjoyed watching them.

28. Most people who are truly happy enjoy their work.

29. The test results that were posted today were a disappointment to some, yet many were happy.

30. As the circus performers paraded down the street, the crowd waved at them and cheered.

31. The train trip that I am taking crosses the Rockies, so it should be very scenic.

32. My mother works as a computer programmer, although she studied library science.

33. After my brother locked his keys in his car, he called for help, which arrived quickly.

34. No one denied that the rain was needed, but many were upset because the fair was rained out.

for CHAPTER 16 page 458 continued

CHAPTER TEST

35. The show, which I never watched, was canceled early in the season.
36. The game had started, and the band was playing, and Dad still had not arrived.
37. Ms. Rosata will help you with the homework whenever you ask her.
38. I like the bread, which is an Italian specialty, so I order it when we go to the restaurant.
39. As the large dog approached, the child became frightened and ran into the house.
40. Maria learned to swim when she was very young, for she always loved being in water, and this is the pool where she learned.

D. IDENTIFYING SENTENCE STRUCTURES On the line provided, identify each of the following sentences by writing *S* for *simple*, *CD* for *compound*, *CX* for *complex*, or *CD-CX* for *compound-complex*.

Example _CD-CX_ 1. Although many book reviewers ignored J. K. Rowling's first book, *Harry Potter and the Sorcerer's Stone*, readers paid attention, and it became a hit.

_____ 41. Because Rowling was an unknown British writer, people did not know what to expect.

_____ 42. The book became popular with readers of all ages, and excitement about it spread.

_____ 43. The first three *Harry Potter* books landed on the bestseller lists because both young people and adults enjoy the stories that follow Harry through his challenging life.

_____ 44. The second novel, *Harry Potter and the Chamber of Secrets*, was eagerly awaited by readers who had become fans of Harry and his adventures.

_____ 45. After the death of his parents, Harry learns that he is a wizard, and he starts attending Hogwarts Academy and learns about his magical powers.

_____ 46. He finds himself among Muggles and is miserable until he finds other non-Muggles like himself.

_____ 47. Rowling plans to write seven books about Harry; there will be one for each year that he is at Hogwarts Academy.

_____ 48. By following the series, young readers can grow up with Harry and proceed through their teen years along with their hero.

_____ 49. In the third book, *The Prisoner of Azkaban*, Harry faces a new action-filled realm of the unknown guarded by a dangerous foe.

_____ 50. No one, except perhaps the author, knows what future adventures await Harry, but millions of readers are eagerly waiting to find out.

Chapter Tests

Agreement: Subject and Verb, Pronoun and Antecedent

A. IDENTIFYING VERBS THAT AGREE IN NUMBER WITH THEIR SUBJECTS In each of the following sentences, underline the correct form of the verb in parentheses.

Example 1. The alligators at the wildlife park (*sleep*, *sleeps*) most of the day.

1. The dulcimer and the fiddle always (*remind*, *reminds*) me of the music we heard when we were in the Appalachians.
2. The new printer in the school office (*make*, *makes*) copies very quickly.
3. (*Don't*, *Doesn't*) any of that politician's views appeal to you?
4. All of the theaters (*is*, *are*) showing mostly the same movies.
5. Ella's blue coat, which has a missing button and three holes, (*remain*, *remains*) her favorite despite how worn it is.
6. (*Have*, *Has*) anyone spoken to you about the concert?
7. Carlos or Jane usually (*know*, *knows*) the answers to most of the questions on the radio's music quiz show.
8. Ecuador (*celebrate*, *celebrates*) its independence on August 10.
9. Your doubts about the water filter (*seem*, *seems*) valid.
10. On the average, only a few people out of a hundred ever (*return*, *returns*) questionnaires that they receive.
11. My sister's shorts (*is*, *are*) in the dryer.
12. Two thirds of the flour (*is*, *are*) still in the bag.
13. Most of the weather report (*is*, *are*) filled with live coverage of the hurricane that has been threatening Florida.
14. The team my two brothers play on (*has*, *have*) won the championship!
15. The chipmunks that I saw last night (*has*, *have*) returned.
16. My dad likes the trapeze artists, but my favorite (*is*, *are*) the clowns.
17. The Philippines (*consist*, *consists*) of more than seven thousand islands.
18. The sound of their voices (*don't*, *doesn't*) carry very far in this fog.
19. Neither my mother nor the parents of my best friend (*like*, *likes*) driving more than fifty miles to and from work.
20. Many of those who work at night (*sleep*, *sleeps*) during the afternoon.

for CHAPTER 17 page 474 continued   CHAPTER TEST

B. Choosing Correct Pronouns and Identifying Antecedents In each of the following sentences, underline the correct pronoun in parentheses. Then, circle its antecedent.

Example 1. The (class) made up (*its*, *their*) own proverbs after hearing recorded passages from Ashley Bryan's book.

21. Alicia read to the class from (*her, their*) copy of Bryan's *The Night Has Ears: African Proverbs*, which she brought from home.
22. *African Proverbs* is a good subtitle because (*it, they*) perfectly describes the book.
23. Many of the stories in the book are so funny that I laughed out loud at (*it, them*).
24. Either Bart or Larry said (*his, their*) favorite proverb is the one about fighting a lion.
25. Mrs. Myers and Alicia agreed that the Swahili proverb is (*her, their*) favorite, too.
26. The artwork that accompanies the stories accurately illustrates (*its, their*) depth and variety.
27. Some proverbs were hard for me to understand until we discussed (*it, them*) in my study group.
28. Alicia read two thirds of the book today, and she promised to finish the rest of (*it, them*) tomorrow.
29. Our class enjoyed (*its, their*) introduction to writings of different cultures.
30. The Friends of the Library also shares (*its, their*) collection of books with us.

C. Proofreading Sentences for Subject-Verb and Pronoun-Antecedent Agreement Most of the following sentences contain an error in agreement. Underline each incorrect verb or pronoun, and write the correct form above it. If a sentence is correct, write *C* on the line provided.

Example _____ 1. The president and chief executive officer are Carlos Perez. *(is above are)*

_____ 31. Five dollars were the price of admission.
_____ 32. Those radios doesn't work anymore, do they?
_____ 33. *Chariots of Fire* are a great movie for runners to see, so you should rent it.
_____ 34. Few of the members in that club is going on the field trip.
_____ 35. There is many beautiful crafts at the show this year.
_____ 36. News can be gloomy, but they also can be uplifting.
_____ 37. Are a wrench or a screwdriver needed to assemble the toy?
_____ 38. Either Tammy or her sisters plans to sing at the assembly.
_____ 39. Saturday afternoons is a good time to go bowling.

Chapter Tests   **75**

for **CHAPTER 17** page 474 continued **CHAPTER TEST**

_____ **40.** Neither the team members nor the coach want to compete in the tournament.

_____ **41.** Those three days during the past several months particularly stands out in my memory.

_____ **42.** Everybody in both Spanish classes have seen the film about Puerto Rico.

_____ **43.** Gloria or one of her aunts intends to bring their wool mittens.

_____ **44.** The team is playing tomorrow at 5 P.M. on its own field.

_____ **45.** Have Franco and Dean shown you their report cards?

_____ **46.** The tickets for the concert tonight is on the table.

_____ **47.** Electronics are a profitable field for employment.

_____ **48.** All of the flowers for the wedding has been delivered to the synagogue.

_____ **49.** Are both of the books lost, or did you find them?

_____ **50.** Your eyeglasses will be easier to see through when you clean it.

NAME _____ CLASS _____ DATE _____ SCORE _____

for **CHAPTER 18** page 504   **CHAPTER TEST**

Using Verbs Correctly: Principal Parts, Regular and Irregular Verbs, Tense, Voice

A. Proofreading Sentences for Correct Verb Forms Most of the following sentences contain errors in the use of verbs. Draw a line through each incorrect verb form, and write the correct form above it. If a sentence is already correct, write *C* on the line provided.

Example _____ 1. The ferret ran into the bedroom and ~~hides~~ *hid* under the bed.

_____ 1. The winds blowed fifty miles an hour during the storm.

_____ 2. The game ended, we put the board and pieces away, and the players goed home.

_____ 3. A few days ago, we seen a raccoon by the cafeteria.

_____ 4. Until you told me, I hadn't knew that Murray is transferring to another school.

_____ 5. Yesterday we studied about Cameroon and learned its location in Africa.

_____ 6. The batter hitted the ball deep into left field.

_____ 7. The prince was crownded in a ceremony in the castle courtyard.

_____ 8. Has the tomato plant grew very much in the new pot?

_____ 9. Three people have spoke to our class about the dangers of smoking.

_____ 10. Mr. Gomez has posted the names of the essay winners on the bulletin board.

_____ 11. The paper carrier has came to our house twice to collect.

_____ 12. The flight attendant has already flew a dozen flights this month.

_____ 13. Jake rided the donkey from the corral to the house.

_____ 14. Andrea use to live in Chinatown in New York City, didn't she?

_____ 15. The pumpkin pies are out of the oven and have began cooling on the rack.

_____ 16. The egg breaked open, and the chick's face appeared.

_____ 17. If we hadn't left the water dripping, the pipes would've froze last night.

_____ 18. The baker brought us three loaves of bread fresh out of the oven.

_____ 19. Lance has wore his lucky shirt to every game this year.

_____ 20. "Someone has drank all of the grape juice," Nan said.

B. Using the Different Tenses of Verbs In each of the following sentences, change the tense of the verb to the tense indicated in parentheses. Underline the original verb form, and write the new form above it.

Example 1. Lori <u>has cut</u> *has been cutting* hair since the age of eight. (*present perfect progressive*)

21. James wrote three e-mails to his friends. (*future perfect*)

Chapter Tests   **77**

for CHAPTER 18 page 504 *continued* **CHAPTER TEST**

22. My sister will learn all the words on the French vocabulary list before the test. (*past perfect*)
23. The team knew their coach's game plan. (*present*)
24. The baby crawls everywhere in the small apartment. (*past emphatic*)
25. How many people had flown with you in the plane? (*past*)
26. The dogs had barked constantly for almost twenty minutes. (*future perfect progressive*)
27. We will go to the farmers' market many times. (*present perfect*)
28. Alinda travels to Argentina once a month. (*future*)
29. The two boys tried on each other's jackets. (*past progressive*)
30. Miss Devoe told funny stories. (*present emphatic*)

C. IDENTIFYING ACTIVE AND PASSIVE VOICE Decide whether the verb in each of the following sentences is in the active or the passive voice. Write *AV* for *active voice* or *PV* for *passive voice* above the verb or verb phrase.

Example 1. Saris have been worn by women in India for centuries. [PV]

31. Since the second century B.C., Indian women have worn saris.
32. Saris traditionally have been made of silk.
33. The colorful saris for sale in this shop were woven by three different men.
34. This sari pattern was designed with a computer.
35. Saris with such designs are top sellers throughout the world.
36. A majority of women in India still wear saris.
37. Many of these garments were traded at the market.
38. India's youth, however, don't always prefer saris.
39. Jeans and T-shirts are sometimes preferred by younger people.
40. Some people wonder about the future of the sari.

D. SPECIAL PROBLEMS WITH VERBS: IDENTIFYING THE CORRECT FORMS OF *SIT* AND *SET*, *LIE* AND *LAY*, *RISE* AND *RAISE* Underline the correct verb in parentheses in each of the following sentences.

Example 1. Theresa has (*lain*, *laid*) the snow globe on the desk.

41. Please (*sit*, *set*) the chair by the window.
42. The snake is (*lying*, *laying*) on the warm sidewalk.
43. Everyone (*rises*, *raises*) when the judge comes into the courtroom.

78 ELEMENTS OF LANGUAGE | Second Course

for CHAPTER 18 page 504 continued **CHAPTER TEST**

44. Mr. Gardner had (*lain, laid*) the stapler on the stack of posters.

45. The sun is (*rising, raising*), so it's time to get up.

46. Grampa is outside (*sitting, setting*) on the porch swing he made last week.

47. My sister had (*risen, raised*) the cover of the terrarium only a little bit, but it was enough to allow the snake to escape.

48. Anne (*lay, laid*) extra blankets at the foot of the bed.

49. Have you (*sat, set*) the groceries on the kitchen counter?

50. Maybe I could (*lie, lay*) down and rest before the party tonight.

for CHAPTER 19 page 534

CHAPTER TEST

Using Pronouns Correctly: Case Forms of Pronouns; Special Pronoun Problems

A. Choosing Correct Pronoun Forms and Identifying Their Case Underline the correct pronoun form in parentheses in each of the following sentences. Then, indicate the case of the pronoun by writing above it *NOM* for nominative, *OBJ* for objective, or *POS* for possessive.

Example 1. The author of that popular novel is (*she*, her). [NOM]

1. The committee members did not know (*who*, *whom*) had won the contest until the judges handed them the envelope.
2. The citizenship award should go to (*they*, *them*).
3. Gloria and (*they*, *them*) delivered the food baskets to the shelter.
4. A friend drove Juwan and (*I*, *me*) to the airport.
5. According to the teacher, my paper and (*your*, *yours*) need to be rewritten.
6. She gave (*we*, *us*) directions to the carnival.
7. The principal chose two people—Judy and (*I*, *me*)—for the new Student Advisory Committee.
8. After the game the players treated (*theirselves*, *themselves*) to a movie.
9. She is the aunt for (*who*, *whom*) I was named.
10. Our new neighbor rode to school with my sister and (*I*, *me*).

B. Choosing Correct Pronoun Forms Underline the correct pronoun form in each of the following sentences.

Example 1. Did you find out (*who*, whom) the guests were?

11. No one in algebra class except (*me*, *I*) knew how to solve the last equation on the quiz.
12. Will Tyler and (*them*, *they*) stay for the whole show?
13. The news delighted (*we*, *us*), to say the least!
14. Angela, (*who*, *whom*) I admire, asked me to help plan the meeting.
15. Have the boys received (*them*, *their*) packages in the mail?
16. The only person I truly trust is (*him*, *he*).
17. The winners—Tara, Brenda, and (*she*, *her*)—were announced this morning.
18. Someone gave (*he*, *him*) a new CD player.
19. My brother and (*me*, *I*) are going hiking this afternoon.
20. "I hope Justin will be joining you and (*I*, *me*) tomorrow," Jeanne said.
21. Please give the apples and oranges to Rick and (*I*, *me*).

80   ELEMENTS OF LANGUAGE | Second Course

| NAME | CLASS | DATE | SCORE |

for CHAPTER 19 page 534 continued   **CHAPTER TEST**

22. Mr. Evans was able to fix the calculator (*himself, hisself*).

23. Dad drove Aunt Sarah and (*she, her*) to the airport.

24. You can tell (*whoever, whomever*) arrives early to wait in the den.

25. The practical jokers could have been (*they, them*).

26. The coach chose only two volunteers, Nora and (*I, me*).

27. Darla and Erwin bought two Chinese boxes for (*themselves, theirselves*).

28. Her bicycle and (*my, mine*) are now in storage.

29. Did the dogs disappear before (*us, we*) opened the door?

30. Just between you and (*I, me*), I don't think anyone can win that game.

C. PROOFREADING SENTENCES FOR CORRECT PRONOUN FORMS Most of the following sentences contain pronouns that have been used incorrectly. Draw a line through each incorrect pronoun, and write the correct form above it. If a sentence is already correct, write *C* on the line provided.

Example _____ 1. The director really gave ~~we~~ *us* band members a workout.

_____ 31. I thought you said you would bring you guitar tonight.

_____ 32. My parents gave themselves a trip to Vietnam for their anniversary.

_____ 33. The ones who know the most about the rules, Jovita and him, missed the game.

_____ 34. Weren't you sitting behind Justin and I in the assembly yesterday?

_____ 35. The principal has called both you and I to her office.

_____ 36. Can anyone tell us whom is knocking at the door?

_____ 37. The guests are indeed making theirselves comfortable.

_____ 38. Do you think the winner should have been him?

_____ 39. Who should we ask for permission to put up campaign posters in the hallways, Ms. Sims?

_____ 40. Our uncle sent my brother and me tickets to the hockey game.

_____ 41. Our team's three swimmers—Juan, Mark, and him—placed first, second, and third in the freestyle competition.

_____ 42. Grandfather called we with the good news.

_____ 43. Does Don speak only for hisself or for his whole club?

_____ 44. You should give him and I directions to the hardware store.

_____ 45. "Whomever is making that noise should stop now!" Ms. Pierce said.

Chapter Tests   **81**

for **CHAPTER 19** page 534 continued   **CHAPTER TEST**

_____ 46. If I am not mistaken, the first ones to cross the finish line were Rob and her.

_____ 47. The song was dedicated to we country music fans.

_____ 48. Jackie always amuses they with her jokes.

_____ 49. For our birthdays, Amber and me want to go to Worlds of Fun.

_____ 50. Please hand the papers either to Carl or I.

for **CHAPTER 20** page 554 **CHAPTER TEST**

Using Modifiers Correctly: Comparison and Placement

A. USING ADJECTIVES AND ADVERBS CORRECTLY IN SENTENCES Underline the correct form of the modifier in parentheses in each of the following sentences.

Example 1. Trisha has a great memory and therefore usually does (good, *well*) when she plays trivia games.

1. The chickens moved (*quick, quickly*) to get out of the way of the cart.
2. The medicine is helping, but Dad still is not (*good, well*) yet.
3. The couple danced (*slow, slowly*) to their favorite tune.
4. The volunteers felt (*good, well*) after a long day's work at the neighborhood park.
5. Our new neighbors seem very friendly and (*nice, nicely*) to me.
6. The bell choir sounded especially (*good, well*) tonight, don't you think?
7. Rhubarb tastes (*sour, sourly*) to me, but it's great mixed with strawberries or cherries.
8. The Trinidad performers certainly played those steel drums (*good, well*).
9. The sudden roar of the big cat was (*unexpected, unexpectedly*) loud.
10. Ramon was dressed very (*professional, professionally*) for his job interview.

B. USING COMPARATIVE AND SUPERLATIVE FORMS CORRECTLY On the line provided, write the correct comparative or superlative form of the modifier given in italics.

Example *little* **1.** Of the two brands of tires, the one on sale is the ___less___ popular.

mild **11.** Everyone is saying that this winter will be _____ than last winter.

much **12.** Although that jar looks smaller, it holds _____ liquid than the other one.

talented **13.** I thought that the acrobats were the _____ of the fifteen or twenty acts we saw at the circus.

much **14.** I already know which of my six classes I will like _____.

hardy **15.** Which is the _____ apple, the Gala or the Jonathan?

brave **16.** Who do you think is the _____ of all the superheroes?

dependable **17.** In my experience, the kind of battery you are planning to buy is the _____ one on the market.

bad **18.** "That is the _____ film I've ever seen!" Zack exclaimed.

available **19.** Fresh produce is perhaps _____ in my area of the state than in yours.

well **20.** Sheila has found that she generally runs _____ in the early morning.

for **CHAPTER 20** page 554 continued

CHAPTER TEST

C. PROOFREADING SENTENCES FOR THE CORRECT USE OF MODIFIERS Each of the following sentences contains an error in the use of modifiers. To correct each sentence, draw a line through the error and, where necessary, write the correction in the space above it. If a sentence requires the addition of a word or words, use a caret (∧) to show where the word or words should be inserted.

Example 1. Alaska is larger than any ∧*other* state in the United States.

21. The painter's self-portrait looked impressively.

22. Of all the dogs we've had, Rex barks loudest and more often.

23. The gorilla is the most powerful and most largest of the great apes.

24. Is San Antonio or Phoenix farthest from your home?

25. After being washed, the quilt is less brighter than it was.

26. The stew tastes gooder tonight than it did last night.

27. Many people don't have no idea where Senegal is.

28. Cora hasn't never eaten sushi, has she?

29. That show quickly became the popularest one on television this season.

30. Mr. Lopez is feeling more better today than he was yesterday.

31. I liked the speaker because she had a positiver attitude than the previous speaker.

32. My friend Grace knows how to search the Internet faster than anyone I know.

33. Cameron has always been least organized than his twin brother.

34. I guess that teacher couldn't hardly understand what we were trying to say.

35. This road is the most straightest one in the county.

36. Nathan plays basketball really good, especially for a beginner.

37. The new print is more clearer than any of the previous ones.

38. As you might expect, Patrice speaks French better than any student at her school.

39. "There isn't nothing you can do about the situation," Mom said.

40. The real estate agent explained the terms of the contract very careful to my mom and dad.

D. CORRECTING DANGLING AND MISPLACED MODIFIERS Most of the following sentences contain dangling or misplaced modifiers. On the line or lines provided, revise each incorrect sentence so that the meaning is clear. If the sentence is already correct, write *C* on the line.

Example 1. The film was about native peoples of the Northwest Coast which we saw in class.

The film, which we saw in class, was about native peoples of the Northwest Coast.

41. Watching the film, the culture of the Chinook, Haida, and other peoples came to life.

| NAME | CLASS | DATE | SCORE |

for CHAPTER 20 page 554 *continued*   **CHAPTER TEST**

42. These groups lived along the Pacific Ocean in the area between southern Alaska and northern California.

43. The ocean of the region and rivers yielded abundant fish and other seafood.

44. Dense forests on steep slopes provided shelter for large animals, including bear, caribou, and moose rising from the beaches.

45. A few families controlled each village with wealth and ancestry.

46. Spending their wealth on food and gifts for guests, feasts called *potlatches* were hosted by families who sought high ranking in villages.

47. Totem poles displayed the titles of the head of the household that stood in front of each home.

48. Great seagoing canoes were crafted by skilled carvers sixty feet or more in length.

49. Iron tools greatly aided the carvers brought by European traders.

50. The Northwest Coast Indians, according to the film, have adapted to change fairly well.

Chapter Tests   **85**

A Glossary of Usage: Common Usage Problems

A. IDENTIFYING CORRECT USAGE Applying the rules of formal, standard English, underline the correct word or word group in parentheses in each of the following sentences.

Example 1. Will the rain (*affect*, *effect*) your decision about going to the game?

1. "It's (*good*, *well*) seeing you again," Uncle Bill said.
2. Earl's knee looks (*bad*, *badly*) now, but the bruise will heal soon.
3. My cousins said (*their*, *there*, *they're*) coming for a visit next summer.
4. I heard (*that*, *where*) the movie *Grizzly Falls* is about a boy who befriends a giant grizzly bear.
5. He (*doesn't*, *don't*) know the price of that action figure yet.
6. The bookshelf is too high to reach (*without*, *unless*) I use a ladder.
7. (*Who's*, *Whose*) that man talking with your father?
8. The music was louder (*than*, *then*) we wanted it to be.
9. Are (*fewer*, *less*) students taking Latin this year?
10. Did your sister (*accept*, *except*) the offer from that new software company?
11. Someone (*should of*, *should have*) asked the new student if he wanted some help finding his way around.
12. Bobby Lee convinced (*hisself*, *himself*) that he was the winner.
13. "I'm (*suppose to*, *supposed to*) be on that train!" Tawanda yelled.
14. We closed the door behind us, (*like*, *as*) we were asked to do.
15. (*It's*, *Its*) too cold in the apartment this morning!
16. The others are (*all ready*, *already*) for the party, but I'm not.
17. "(*Try and*, *Try to*) be on time, please," Mrs. Mulligan said.
18. You may want to copy (*them*, *those*) letters to your save file.
19. Annabelle is the horse (*that*, *who*) Carrie likes best.
20. A powwow is a ceremony (*between*, *among*) North American Indians.
21. We looked (*everywhere*, *everywheres*) for my stepsister's mitten but never found it.
22. (*Your*, *You're*) package arrived before Eva's birthday, didn't it?
23. What (*affect*, *effect*) do you think the news will have?
24. My grandpa (*learned*, *taught*) me how to use the compass he gave me.
25. Shoe prices have dropped (*somewhat*, *some*) since spring.

B. Proofreading for Correct Usage Most of the following sentences contain an error in the use of formal, standard English. If a sentence contains an error in usage, rewrite the sentence correctly on the line provided. If the sentence is already correct, write C on the line.

Example 1. Could you take a few games for us to play when you come to visit?

Could you bring a few games for us to play when you come to visit?

26. A coronation is a ceremony where a ruler is crowned.

27. Would you please bring the canned goods to the shelter when you go?

28. We're learning alot about Frederick Douglass from his autobiography.

29. It's going to be dark in less than a hour.

30. At the assembly the committee had ought to present the plan for the fall festival.

31. At first our new cat acted like we didn't exist.

32. Everyone can go except Carla and Janis.

33. The balloon busted as soon as it hit the tree.

34. Many people seem to like these kind of fabrics for shirts this year.

35. Did all three of your uncles buy theirselves some red suspenders?

36. Chihuahua, Mexico, is a long ways from Toronto, Canada.

37. My parents probably will leave me go on the field trip unless they change their minds.

for CHAPTER 21 page 580 *continued*

CHAPTER TEST

38. "I can't hardly wait for you to see my new computer system," Kim said.

39. Do you think we have enough lemonade to fill this here pitcher?

40. My friend he went to visit his grandmother in Oklahoma.

41. Maybe the flight attendant knows who's suitcase this is.

42. "Where is the museum at?" Lorna asked.

43. How come people don't look on the bright side of things more of the time?

44. Let's go inside of the cabin to get warm.

45. Even the coach is kind of tired after the long practice session this afternoon.

46. India ain't in Europe, but Spain and Greece are.

47. Live oaks don't lose all they're leaves each winter.

48. You can tell that the dog really misses it's owner.

49. The boys are all right despite hiking for miles in the rain.

50. The reason Holly Robinson Peete is featured in the article is because she was honored by the Rainbow/PUSH Coalition.

for **CHAPTER 22** page 602

CHAPTER TEST

Capital Letters: Rules for Capitalization

A. CORRECTING ERRORS IN CAPITALIZATION Most of the following items contain at least one error in capitalization. If an item contains an error, write the item with correct capitalization on the line provided. If an item is already correct, write *C* on the line.

Example 1. minerva, a roman Goddess   *Minerva, a Roman goddess*

1. a tony award
2. interested in hinduism
3. on mother's day
4. the dallas cowboys
5. in math class
6. the chisholm trail
7. his other Aunt
8. captain Joe Dupont
9. some lipton tea
10. Carnegie Hall in New York City
11. an ethiopian city
12. the constellation gemini
13. the launch of *viking 1*
14. the movie *Toy Story*
15. an american indian story
16. The day has come, father.
17. Socialist philosophy
18. the national wildlife federation
19. a beautiful Fall day
20. my horse, trotter

B. USING CAPITAL LETTERS CORRECTLY In each of the following sentences, underline each word that should begin with a capital letter.

Example 1. When he was a boy, <u>mr.</u> Griffin lived on <u>fifty-ninth</u> <u>street</u> near the <u>mississippi</u> <u>river</u>.

21. My first line in the play began "o noble king Rowse, whose wit is brighter than venus."

22. Our new pet, purry, is a persian cat that adopted us near the sinclair plaza in february.

Chapter Tests **89**

NAME _____ CLASS _____ DATE _____ SCORE _____

for CHAPTER 22 **page 602** *continued* **CHAPTER TEST**

23. In typing 1, miss cornack told us to end business letters with "sincerely yours."

24. The governor referred to wycrest academy as one of the best public schools in the midwest and presented the 2000 excellence in education award to the principal.

25. "I look forward to seeing you on tuesday," aunt irene said. "perhaps you could even come this evening, if you have time."

26. In his job at consolidated trucking co., Bob routinely drives interstate 35 from des moines, iowa, to fort worth, texas.

27. is earth closer to the sun than mars or jupiter is?

28. My friend ruth's family always observes purim, a holiday that celebrates Esther's success in saving many jews from being massacred.

29. oh, animated films such as *princess Mononoke* by the director hayao miyazaki are extremely popular with japanese audiences and others all over the world.

30. According to an ad in *reader's digest*, toyota trucks have been built in brazil since 1959.

C. PROOFREADING FOR CORRECT USE OF CAPITAL LETTERS Each of the following sentences contains at least one error in capitalization. Correct each error by crossing out the incorrect letter and writing the correct form above it.

Example 1. My ~~M~~om and ~~D~~ad were in ~~g~~alveston, ~~t~~exas, when ~~h~~urricane Alicia hit there in 1983.
(corrections above: m, d, G, T, H)

31. Nations belonging to the world meteorological organization select what names will be given to hurricanes each year.

32. Of course, mom knew that Forecasters began giving storms female names during world war II.

33. yesterday, we learned in Science class that men's names were added in 1978.

34. Carlos wrote to the national oceanic and atmospheric administration to get more information about hurricane names.

35. Did anyone in your Class know that the national hurricane center in miami, florida, assigns the names?

36. The six lists from which names are chosen can be found in reference sources about the Weather, including *chase's 2000 calendar of events*.

37. For example, in 2001, the eastern pacific names include adolph, kiko, manuel, and velma.

38. my Cousin Bill, who is studying Meteorology, said that the names of severe storms (such as iniki, which caused great damage in hawaii) are not used again.

90 ELEMENTS OF LANGUAGE | Second Course

for CHAPTER 22 page 602 continued **CHAPTER TEST**

39. Our class visited a Science Museum near here to see the exhibit about hurricanes that have hit States along the gulf of mexico.

40. One of my Aunts, marta, and one of my Uncles, laurence, had their names used for Storms.

D. Correcting Errors in Capitalization Each of the following sentences contains at least one error in capitalization. Correct each error by crossing out the incorrect letter and writing the correct form above it.

Example 1. The catalogue published this ~~W~~inter features books by and about ~~a~~frican Americans.
                                                          w   A

41. I'm doing my book report on Jane goodall's book *Africa in my blood: an autobiography in letters*.

42. My Uncle Lou says that we had ancestors at the 1893 columbian exposition.

43. Our Science teacher ordered a copy of *Black women scientists in the United States* to use in class.

44. one book my friend eric plans to get is *Hip Hop America*, which covers the history of hip hop since the 1970's.

45. One of the best sources I found for information about music of Africa and the orient was a book by otto karolyi.

46. Both mrs. Murphy and i are eager to read about the slave ship *henrietta marie*, the only slave ship that has ever been found.

47. Willie Mays, the famous san francisco giants outfielder, is the subject of a new rhyming story.

48. In a book from the university press of Florida, Idella Parker tells about working with Author Marjorie Kinnan Rawlings, who won a pulitzer prize.

49. Jane McManus describes the lives of cuban residents, especially those from the isle of pines during the 1900's.

50. At our wednesday night bible study meeting, reverend Maday said *A History of the church in Africa* is an interesting account of the rise of christianity in that part of the Earth.

Chapter Tests

NAME	CLASS	DATE	SCORE

for CHAPTER 23 page 628 **CHAPTER TEST**

Punctuation: End Marks, Commas, Semicolons, and Colons

A. CORRECTING SENTENCES BY ADDING END MARKS Insert end marks (periods, exclamation points, and question marks) where they are needed in the following sentences.

Example 1. Hand me a sheet of that paper, please.

1. What beautiful stationery you have
2. It's banana paper, which actually contains banana fibers
3. Where do you get banana paper
4. Alexandra bought the paper for me when she was in Costa Rica
5. Wow, that's a neat present
6. Please tell us more about banana paper
7. Earth College in Costa Rica processes the paper
8. Isn't the fiber a byproduct of the banana harvest
9. Do profits from some banana paper go to Latin American students
10. The sale of banana paper helps make it possible for Earth College students to learn about ways to sustain agricultural growth in Latin America

B. CORRECTING SENTENCES BY ADDING PERIODS Insert periods where they are needed for abbreviations in the following sentences.

Example 1. J.T. Larimer lives at 947 Coltraine St.

11. Ms Donelevy now works for the Rankin Co, I'm told.
12. Dan Pate, Jr, who was a longtime FBI agent, moved to Hot Springs, Ark, last year after he retired.
13. Deborah is just right for the part in the play because she is 5 ft 9 in tall.
14. The test began promptly at 9 A M, but only two people took it.
15. Is your new address 81 Plaza Ave, Atlanta, GA 30327?
16. Dr. R L Madison, who still makes house calls, arrived at 6:30 P M.
17. Both St. Louis and Ft Madison are located on the Missouri River.
18. Have you ever wondered what life was like in the sixth century B C ?
19. Our VCR was broken for a month until Mrs Lee fixed it.
20. You can send the package to me at P O Box 1187 after next week.

92 ELEMENTS OF LANGUAGE | Second Course

for **CHAPTER 23** page 628 continued   **CHAPTER TEST**

C. Correcting Sentences by Adding Commas Insert commas where they are needed in the following sentences. If a sentence is already correct, write *C* on the line provided.

Example _____ **1.** The fjord,a narrow arm of the sea,lies between steep,rocky cliffs.

_____ **21.** Exhausted from her tennis match Zia rested before going to the concert.

_____ **22.** I doubt that you will ever forget winning the game on April 2, 1999, nor will I.

_____ **23.** Although everyone else in his family was born in the spring Ralph ever his own person was born in November.

_____ **24.** We're not sure where the wildlife park is what time it opens or when it closes.

_____ **25.** Martha please answer the telephone while I'm vacuuming.

_____ **26.** The store in my opinion was too crowded so we didn't look around very long.

_____ **27.** The weather was cold cloudy and snowy but they still enjoyed their walk.

_____ **28.** Yes my grandparents moved last month to Jackson Wyoming.

_____ **29.** The gerberas which are among my favorite plants have orange pink white and violet flowers.

_____ **30.** I think that the gray coat I need is in the hall closet or still in my locker at school.

D. Using Semicolons Correctly in Sentences Insert semicolons where they are needed in the following sentences. If the sentence already contains a comma or another punctuation mark where the semicolon should go, delete the punctuation mark in the sentence, and write the semicolon above it.

Example 1. The waiter recited the daily specials to Fran, Dexter, and Orion;/and Sarah and I overheard at a nearby table.

31. That red shirt is my best silk shirt, in fact, it is my only silk shirt.

32. The bagels were a big hit everybody enjoyed the extra raisins in them.

33. On Tuesday we toured San Rafael, on Wednesday we boated on San Francisco Bay.

34. "I'm busy tomorrow night, otherwise, I'd love to go with you," Lynn said.

35. The documentary focused on artwork in Florence, Italy, Paris, France, and London, England.

36. Rebecca is very good with numbers, consequently, she excels in math classes.

37. The building was begun on January 3, 1997, completed on February 3, 1998, and opened on March 3, 1998.

38. Thad repaired his bicycle yesterday, his sister, therefore, was able to ride it today.

Chapter Tests

39. The new choir members are Carol, Kenneth, and Robert, and Sophie, Allen, and Cathy are alternate members.

40. I paid full price for my ticket, they bought their tickets at half price, however.

E. Correcting Sentences by Adding Colons Insert colons where they are needed in the following sentences. Circle any lowercase letters that should be capital letters. If a sentence does not need a colon, write *C* on the line provided.

Example _____ **1.** The relay race has been rescheduled. (t)he new time is 1 P.M.

_____ **41.** One of my main sources of information was *Native American Women A Biographical Dictionary*.

_____ **42.** Make sure you have the following materials with you for the test tomorrow two sharpened pencils, a protractor, a ruler, and a compass.

_____ **43.** Sondra had one lifelong ambition she wanted to work for the United Nations.

_____ **44.** "The movie begins at 1 40 P.M., and I do not want to be late," Maggie said.

_____ **45.** Your information can come from the library, newspapers, or the Internet.

_____ **46.** The order of your classes will be as follows speech, math, English, science, and gym.

_____ **47.** Jan, you are now the leading candidate, and the election is only two weeks away.

_____ **48.** Renewing the mind is the theme of the Biblical verse in Romans 12 2.

_____ **49.** Joshua is qualified to be club president he has served as vice-president for two years.

_____ **50.** The speaker finished with these words "Remember that your own thoughts and feelings can affect your experiences. Do yourself a favor and lighten up."

NAME _____ CLASS _____ DATE _____ SCORE _____

for **CHAPTER 24** page 658   **CHAPTER TEST**

Punctuation: Underlining (Italics), Quotation Marks, Apostrophes, Hyphens, Parentheses, Brackets, Dashes

A. USING UNDERLINING (ITALICS) CORRECTLY IN SENTENCES Underline the word, words, or other items that should be italicized in each of the following sentences.

Example 1. There is no <u>r</u> in the second syllable of the word <u>sherbet</u>.

1. The numbers 3 and 6 have been in every address Sheila has had.
2. Maria Del Rey's recording Lullabies of Latin America is available at the library.
3. Among the Amtrak trains that cross the West are the California Zephyr and the Texas Eagle.
4. The oil painting Cupcake in the new exhibit features a cow that looks like the one I raised for my Future Farmers of America project.
5. Was the article on mapmaking in Navigator or in Car and Driver magazine?
6. The movie Sleepy Hollow is loosely based on a classic Washington Irving tale.
7. Notice that the word necessary contains one c but two s's.
8. Captain James Cook reached Australia in his ship Endeavour in April 1770.
9. Mr. Sims took flying lessons in planes named Wings and Wings II.
10. One of the best books I've read about the life of musicians on the road is titled The Big Wheel.

B. PUNCTUATING SENTENCES BY ADDING QUOTATION MARKS In the following sentences, insert quotation marks and single quotation marks where they are needed. Circle any lowercase letters that should be capital letters. If a sentence is already correct, write C on the line provided.

Example _____ **1.** Carlos asked, "(i)s the poem 'Mist Over Paris' in that book?"

_____ 11. Someone is knocking at the door, Dylan said. It is probably Uncle Ray.

_____ 12. Quick, help! Angela screamed. I'm dropping the jars of paint!

_____ 13. Actor Robin Williams said, my father told me I should always have a backup profession like welding.

_____ 14. Mrs. Meyer said that we all passed the test with flying colors.

_____ 15. I didn't see the Rescued on Ice episode, he said. I haven't watched much TV lately.

_____ 16. What, Leigh asked, is the reason for your decision?

_____ 17. Carl replied, no one knows these mountains better than I do.

_____ 18. I really like the novel, Brad said, and my favorite chapter is Wild Ride.

_____ 19. In the movie, who says Together we can win? Marge asked.

_____ 20. How many of you know the words to the song Count Your Pennies?

Chapter Tests   **95**

for CHAPTER 24 page 658 continued

CHAPTER TEST

C. Punctuating Dialogue by Adding Quotation Marks Insert quotation marks where they are needed in the following dialogue. (Note: All sentences are dialogue, including those for which no speaker is given.)

Example 1. "Many countries have satellites and other space objects in orbit," Ms. Powell said.

21. Wow! Alicia said. I've never thought much about how many objects must be out there in orbit.

22. There are quite a few, actually. In fact, as of 1999, the number was 8,820, Ms. Powell said.

23. I know what satellites are, Trevor said, but what do you mean when you say 'space objects'?

24. Space objects include debris, such as parts of rockets that came off during launching or later when the rockets were destroyed, Ms. Powell said.

25. NASA keeps detailed records of what is up in orbit and what country put each object there.

26. Does that include countries in Asia? Alicia asked.

27. Yes, they are well represented, Ms. Powell replied.

28. India, for example, she continued, had nineteen satellites and five objects of debris.

29. Other countries include Indonesia with eight satellites, South Korea with five, Thailand with four, and Japan with sixty-five satellites, four space probes, and fifty-one objects of debris.

30. You can find up-to-date information about these orbiting objects by visiting the Space Objects Box Score Web site, Mrs. Powell suggested.

D. Correcting Sentences by Adding Apostrophes Insert apostrophes where they are needed in the following sentences. If a sentence is already correct, write *C* on the line provided.

Example _____ **1.** In the story, the mice's unexpected friend isn't the cat, but the ferret.

_____ 31. "There are too many *I*s in your report, Daniel," Mr. Dodson said.

_____ 32. Its a beautiful day; dont spoil it by worrying.

_____ 33. Whos going to the ballets opening performance?

_____ 34. The mens department is having a sale starting at one o clock this afternoon.

_____ 35. The 1990s was an exciting decade of technological advances, wasnt it?

_____ 36. The horses heads turned in anticipation when they heard Sarahs voice.

_____ 37. The society appreciates everyones help in distributing the toys.

_____ 38. This purse is yours, but hers is very similar.

_____ 39. Theyve answered all the questions, but now we cant find their tests.

_____ 40. The cars engine is running great, but its body needs repair.

96 ELEMENTS OF LANGUAGE | Second Course

for CHAPTER 24 page 658 continued **CHAPTER TEST**

E. Using Hyphens, Parentheses, Brackets, and Dashes Correctly in Sentences Insert hyphens, parentheses, brackets, and dashes to punctuate the following sentences correctly. Use a caret (∧) to indicate where each punctuation mark should go. Do not add commas to these sentences.

Example 1. Give me —oh, I mean us— two-thirds cup of potato soup.

41. The restaurant's menu much to my surprise is all dairy free.

42. Three fourths of the players on my grandfather's softball team are over seventy five years old.

43. In his speech the senator said, "This event the opening of this new expressway will for ever change the area."

44. Cyrus II 585–529 B.C. is a well known king who founded the Persian Empire.

45. John's grandmother grew up in Yuma, Arizona, where she first met his grand father, who moved there in 1957 from Mexico City.

46. The chukar chə·kär´ is a partridge introduced into the United States from Asia and Europe.

47. "It's important to have good self esteem and believe in one's own abilities," the speaker said.

48. The announcer said, "And the winner is do you *really* want to know?"

49. Expresident George Bush had two sons serving as governors of southern states at the end of the last century.

50. The film is about an adventurous American Revolutionary soldier (Daniel Shays 1747–1825).

for **CHAPTER 25** page 686

CHAPTER TEST

Spelling: Improving Your Spelling

A. CORRECTING ERRORS IN SPELLING AND IN WRITING NUMBERS Most of the following sentences contain at least one error in spelling or in writing numbers. Cross out each error, and write the word or number correctly above the error. If a sentence is already correct, write *C* on the line provided.

Example _____ 1. The engineers ~~beleive~~ *believe* the rock wall was built ~~3000~~ *three thousand* years ago.

_____ 1. 4,000 cheering fans rose to their feet for the exciting final minute of the game.

_____ 2. Naomi dreamed about two toyes that built a rocket to Mars.

_____ 3. The editor in chiefs of the two newspapers compared their storys of the event.

_____ 4. *Mahabharata* is 1 of the most beautiful masterpeices of literature and religion in India.

_____ 5. We're looking forward to the ninth grade, which will be our first year in high school.

_____ 6. The legislators proceded to overide the president's veto.

_____ 7. Neither of the girls can walk comfortably in her new shoes.

_____ 8. A Vietnamese family who moved here last July has openned two new businesses that we are very glad to have in our community.

_____ 9. Many of the rooves in our nieghborhood are made of Spanish tile.

_____ 10. I love to sing in the choir, but I rarly do soloes.

_____ 11. For beginers, those three art students are excellent painters.

_____ 12. Both Ned and Victoria often bring their banjos to our beach partys.

_____ 13. The new building requirements have superseded the ones that were in effect when my father began our room addition.

_____ 14. For the 3rd year in a row, Roberta Clary and the rest of the Claries attended Native Americans' Day in South Dakota.

_____ 15. Our pop quizes in spelling can be rather challenging.

_____ 16. I think this letter came back to you because the two 7s in the address look like 9s.

_____ 17. Some people love potatos so much that they eat them almost dayly.

_____ 18. Don't all fives-year-old need to be accompanied by an adult when they are around the pool?

_____ 19. My friend Claire is reading a book about African American business leaders.

_____ 20. We sold a total of one hundred twenty-two tickets to the Shakespeare festival our little theater group put on in October.

for CHAPTER 25 page 686 continued

CHAPTER TEST

_____ 21. The sheep all cryed out noisily as the barking dog herded them through the gate.

_____ 22. The dog was baying at the moon, and the gooses were honking at the dog.

_____ 23. The childs liked playing with the brightly colored dishs from Peru.

_____ 24. Did you see last night's game? The final play was unbelieveable!

_____ 25. How many movie videoes do you usualy rent in a month?

B. DISTINGUISHING BETWEEN WORDS OFTEN CONFUSED Underline the correct word in each set of parentheses in the following sentences.

Example 1. Zach's (*advice*, *advise*) is not to let the game's outcome (*effect*, *affect*) your mood.

26. The (*principle*, *principal*) (*lead*, *led*) the new students down the hall to the library.

27. The Japanese plum, a tree native (*to*, *too*) China, has (*quiet*, *quite*) beautiful fruit.

28. Although the combat troops grew (*weak*, *week*) from hunger and exhaustion, none of them (*deserted*, *desserted*).

29. The cousins were (*all together*, *altogether*) for Aunt Rowana's birthday (*hear*, *here*) at our house.

30. If you could be (*consul*, *counsel*) of any country, what country would you (*choose*, *chose*)?

31. Since the (*weather*, *whether*) is expected to be sunny in San Jose, be sure to take (*your*, *you're*) sunscreen.

32. I had a (*peace*, *piece*) of banana bread for (*desert*, *dessert*).

33. The tower (*shown*, *shone*) in the distance as the caravan approached it from the (*desert*, *dessert*).

34. An indoor (*stationary*, *stationery*) bike can provide good exercise when (*its*, *it's*) raining outside.

35. The (*capital*, *capitol*) is built of limestone that came from a quarry that is not (*to*, *too*, *two*) far from here.

36. The school (*counselor*, *councilor*) told me that I should take algebra rather (*then*, *than*) geometry.

37. Have you (*all ready*, *already*) been to the Ethiopian restaurant, where customers are encouraged to eat with (*there*, *their*) fingers?

38. The church (*alter*, *altar*) was decorated for our vigil for world (*piece*, *peace*).

39. (*Whether*, *Weather*) or not you like parsley, it nicely (*complements*, *compliments*) many entrees.

40. Both boys and girls enrolled in the (*coarse*, *course*) to learn how to make (*clothes*, *cloths*) for themselves.

Chapter Tests

99

for CHAPTER 25 page 686 continued

CHAPTER TEST

41. The (*plane, plain*) landed in Monrovia, the (*capital, capitol*) of Liberia, ahead of schedule.

42. Ashley, (*formally, formerly*) the (*quiet, quite*) member of our group, now is very talkative.

43. "(*Whose, Who's*) the longest-serving member on the city (*council, counsel*)?" the reporter asked.

44. "If the pants are too (*loose, lose*) at the (*waist, waste*), put on a belt," Mom said.

45. "No (*compliment, complement*), sincerely given, is ever (*waisted, wasted*)," the speaker told the crowd.

46. The mayor (*accepted, excepted*) the large drum, made and used by the Osage, during a ceremony last (*weak, week*).

47. My friends (*adviced, advised*) me to stop worrying because everything would be (*alright, all right*).

48. Aaron (*choose, chose*) the (*stationary, stationery*) that had pictures of sports gear all around the edges.

49. Jay applied the (*break, brake*) when he saw the sign, "You just (*passed, past*) the park entrance."

50. The new highway will mainly go (*threw, through*) rural land east of town and will not (*affect, effect*) many residents or businesses.

| NAME | CLASS | DATE | SCORE |

for **CHAPTER 26** page 716   **CHAPTER TEST**

Correcting Common Errors: Key Language Skills Review

A. CORRECTING SENTENCE FRAGMENTS AND RUN-ON SENTENCES Each of the following word groups is a sentence fragment, a run-on sentence, or a complete sentence. Identify each word group by writing on the line provided *F* for *fragment*, *R* for *run-on*, or *S* for a *complete sentence*. Correct each fragment by adding or deleting a word or words to make a complete sentence. Correct each run-on by making it into two separate sentences or by using a word or words to combine the two parts of the run-on to make one complete sentence. Punctuation and capitalization will need to be changed in some cases.

                                                                             and

Example   _R_   **1.** Bolivia is almost in the middle of South America,~~it~~ shares borders with five other countries.

_____ **1.** Surrounded by Brazil, Paraguay, Argentina, Chile, and Peru.

_____ **2.** Of course, Bolivia has no seacoast it does have many other interesting natural features.

_____ **3.** Within Bolivia's borders lie the Andes Mountains and tropical rain forests.

_____ **4.** When I read about Bolivia's grasslands and swamps.

_____ **5.** Bolivia was first populated by American Indians.

_____ **6.** Spain ruled the area for several hundred years in 1825 Bolivia gained independence.

_____ **7.** Was named for the Venezuelan general Simón Bolívar.

_____ **8.** A country that is known for its tin production?

_____ **9.** Bolivia has three official languages about one third of the population speak Spanish.

_____ **10.** The other two thirds speak Aymara and Quechua, both of which are native languages.

B. CORRECTING USAGE ERRORS IN SENTENCES Draw a line through the incorrect word or words in each of the following sentences. Then, write the correct word or words above each error. In some cases, you will simply need to add or delete a word or words to correct an error.

                     drove through

Example 1. The artist ~~drived threw~~ the Ozarks, where she photographed the ~~most~~ oldest houses, barns, and other structures she saw.

11. Our plans for the picnic was almost cancelled after Jean and Simon changed there minds.

12. Mario use to play the piano good, but he can't now because he don't practice.

13. When the snow began to fall yesterday, we brung the plants inside where its more warm.

14. If the two actors in the play wants these props, they should of already told me theirselves.

15. Mrs. Baird she was my most best teacher last year; she was especially nice to my sister and I.

16. That singer, whom stars on Broadway, is popular, but two thirds of my friends hasn't never heard of her.

17. Raj, my stuffed toy tiger, is larger then any stuffed animal setting on the shelves in my room.

Chapter Tests   **101**

| NAME | CLASS | DATE | SCORE |

for CHAPTER 26 page 716 *continued* **CHAPTER TEST**

18. Each of the club members accept two, he and she, are all ready eligible for the prize.

19. Nancy and me can see much more far with the binoculars, which is easy to adjust, than we had thought we could.

20. Here's the vegetable seeds for you're fall garden, along with an free spade.

21. Neither the police captain nor the officers expects the new station to be finished before May unless the winter is more mild than last year.

22. Please give he the cards so that he can distribute them, and everyone can have their own.

23. The Netherlands are located in northwestern Europe, which is a long ways from my home.

24. If her temperature raises, Mom and Betty wants to be notified.

25. The person to call with the test results is him; however, he usually don't get home until six P.M.

C. REVISING SENTENCES TO CORRECT MISPLACED AND DANGLING MODIFIERS Each of the following sentences contains a misplaced or dangling modifier. Revise each sentence to correct the error.

Example 1. The light strip is out on the back porch that needs new bulbs.
The light strip that needs new bulbs is out on the back porch..

26. Dad found some old photographs looking through his file cabinet.

27. Fleeing the winter storm, the sky was filled with migrating geese.

28. When we lived closer to town, I nearly heard the chimes every hour.

29. Aunt Evelyn asked me to visit her next month when she was here for Thanksgiving.

30. The book came from the downtown library, which is due tomorrow.

31. Knowing it would be cold in St. Paul, lots of winter clothes were packed in Jill's suitcase.

32. I almost have read all of *The Prince and the Pauper*, but I have a few pages remaining.

33. The package was from the Walshes that arrived in the mail today from Honolulu.

for **CHAPTER 26** page 716 continued   **CHAPTER TEST**

34. Even though they bark a lot, Paul and his family want to keep all the puppies.

_____

35. Seated in the fifth row, all of the actors' dialogue could be heard clearly.

_____

D. CORRECTING MECHANICS ERRORS IN SENTENCES The following sentences contain errors in capitalization, punctuation, or spelling. Draw a line through each error, and write the correct word or punctuation mark above the error. In some cases, you will simply need to add or delete punctuation. Underline any words that should be in italics.

                        three   *here*

Example 1. "The ~~3~~ new staff members ~~hear~~ are Jim, Stacy**,** and Ann**;** and Jessica, Kevin, and

Marla are helping them learn what to do," said Charlene**.**

36. Its the principal in this situation that truely matters Jessica said

37. Were you disappointed when the councilor said that you need 5 more credits, including Biology?

38. By 5 P M i need to buy the following supplies two wrenches fluid for the breaks on my moms car and an oil filter.

39. If you cant find a plastic sliegh the right hieght for the display let me know perhaps I can find one at the hobby store on collins street just passed my house.

40. "Yes Im sure that we will want to go too the concert next weak," exclaimed Rayna

41. the art students recieved a boost this summer they placed 2nd in the contest sponsored by arteen supplies unlimited during july.

42. My favorite passage in the Bible on joyfulness is Psalm 16 11, Norma said.

43. Marcus' father a well respected chef owns that italian restaurant but I rarely see him their.

44. How to Find True Freedom is a long difficult chapter yet its discussion of world piece is definitely worth reading.

45. oh, weve missed the plain, Kerry said and the last train runs at 1 48 P M

46. This stationary is your's I believe ms Lyons.

47. 300 acres are for sale between jones middle school and mt pleasant drive.

48. Every evening, we take the puppys for a walk threw the park near the lincoln bridge

49. Brent asked who are the heros in you're life Erica

50. My Dad all ready had excepted the job in Washington D C however he postponed the starting date until after my brothers graduation party.

Chapter Tests   **103**